TILLICH

ABINGDON PILLARS
OF THEOLOGY

TILLICH

DONALD W. MUSSER AND
JOSEPH L. PRICE

Abingdon Press
Nashville

TILLICH

Copyright © 2010 by Abingdon Press

All rights reserved.

This book is printed on acid-free paper.

Library of Congress Cataloging-in-Publication Data

Musser, Donald W., 1942-
  Tillich / Donald W. Musser and Joseph L. Price.
    p. cm. — (Abingdon pillars of theology)
  Includes bibliographical references and index.
  ISBN 978-0-687-34344-7 (pbk. : alk. paper)
1. Tillich, Paul, 1886-1965. I. Price, Joseph L., 1949- II. Title.
  BX4827.T53M87 2010
  230.092—dc22

                                                                    2009020527

All scripture quotations are taken from the New Revised Standard Version of the Bible, copyright 1989, Division of Christian Education of the National Council of the Churches of Christ in the United States of America. Used by permission. All rights reserved.

10 11 12 13 14 15 16 17 18 19—10 9 8 7 6 5 4 3 2 1

MANUFACTURED IN THE UNITED STATES OF AMERICA

To the memory of our teacher,

Langdon B. Gilkey

February 9, 1919–November 19, 2004

And to the memory of our classmate and friend,

John Powell Clayton

April 18, 1943–September 21, 2003

Tillich scholars both, who lived lives of courage

CONTENTS

PREFACE

At the end of the first decade of the twenty-first century, when new technological and political futures emerge almost daily, and the twentieth century seems as if it occurred almost a millennium ago, a brief *apologia* may be in order to justify the abiding relevance of a theologian whose pen was silenced in 1965 yet whose inclusion in this theological series is regarded as a pillar. The answer, briefly, is that his voice remains heard in the academic world of seminary and university courses, in essays and books that both engage and reference his work, in the life of the churches where his three volumes of sermons still inform and inspire contemporary preachers, and in the wider culture where, often inchoately, questions of the meaning of life, nature, and history beg for cognitive and moral perspectives that inform and provide the hope for new *kairoi*.

In light of the expansiveness of his influence, it is with some trepidation that we undertake the venture of trying to convey Paul Tillich's ideas and insights in such short space. Nonetheless, in this slim volume we endeavor to achieve two goals. First, we aim to produce a readable, yet theologically savvy rendering of his major works and ideas. Readers accustomed to the "sound-byte" generation should be warned that this goal does not presage an easier and simpler Tillich, because his work does not lend itself to simplification. Readers must plunge into the sea of his thinking, flounder at first, immerse themselves in it, and then, we hope, get hooked by its structures and contents, by its vigor and rigor. We have provided some deliberate redundancies in the text and an extensive lexicon to assist swimmers who need the aid of a text-vest.

Second, while seeking to describe and illumine his work, we point toward Tillich's relevance to today's churches and global culture. For us, a number of his emphases, especially with regard to the creative roles of faith in culture, are striking.

ACKNOWLEDGMENTS

A great cloud of witnesses hovers over this volume. We want to acknowledge them and offer our sincere thanks for their contributions.

For more than two decades we have had an amicable and fruitful relationship with editors, managers, and marketers at Abingdon Press's Academic Books division, who previously worked in tandem with us to bring to text two theological handbooks. Our present publication has been ably nurtured by the guidance, encouragement, and patience of our editor, Kathy Armistead.

We have been taught by some of the most noted theorists and theologians at the intersection of religion and culture. They enabled our ability to write this volume. While we pursued our graduate degrees, in common we shared in the guidance and inspiration provided by our professors Langdon Gilkey, David Tracy, Brian Gerrish, Eric Rust, James Leo Garrett, and Franz Bibfeldt. Among Joe's other teachers, he notes particularly Nathan A. Scott Jr., David Mueller, Dale Moody, Burton Cooper, Alan Gragg, and Harold Wahking. Don notes among his other teachers Philip Hefner, Joseph Sittler, and George Kehm. For a decade, Don has taught a seminar on Tillich at Stetson University. His learning how to engage Tillich at the entry level has been fostered by students in this course, especially Kevin Boyd, Wesley Sun, John Mills, Christine Hinton, Timothy Reddish, Elizabeth Reddish Wright, Kevin Robert Gordon Hanson, Jamie Haskins, Alicia Hickman, Ken Matthews, Tara Holcomb, and Amy Farrell. At various points in his courses at Whittier College and in adult education classes in churches throughout the Los Angeles area, Joe has challenged students with *The Dynamics of Faith* and *The Courage to Be*. His enthusiasm for introducing Tillich to them has been intensified by numerous students and colleagues, including Pamela Hill, Ramon Arrowsmith, Kent Gilbert, Colleen Windham, and Taisha Bonilla.

A wider audience also deserves our appreciation. Our spouses, Bonnie and Ruth, have unfettered us from familial tasks and freed us to collaborate in isolated locales, including a cabin in Fairdealing, Kentucky, thanks to the kindness of its owner, E. Anne Price. Friends Ed and Ruth B. Shannon also supported the final stages by providing a writing retreat in the Eastern Sierras. Lisa Guenther, senior secretary at Stetson University, brought scrawled and cryptic longhand drafts to camera-ready master pages. Alicia Hickman, Sarah Reed Jay, and Candace Hall Doughty gave us grammatical and conceptual critiques on parts of the manuscript, and Katy Simonian assisted in proofreading and preparing the index. Our friend and colleague Dixon Sutherland gave us more advice than we expected, especially from his vast knowledge of the European context of Tillich's life and work.

ABBREVIATIONS

BR   *Biblical Religion and the Search for Ultimate Reality.* Chicago: University of Chicago Press, 1955.

CB   *The Courage to Be.* New Haven: Yale University Press, 1952.

CE   *Christianity and the Encounter of the World Religions.* New York: Columbia University Press, 1963.

DF   *The Dynamics of Faith.* New York: Harper & Brothers, 1957.

EN   *The Eternal Now.* New York: Charles Scribner's Sons, 1963.

FR   *The Future of Religions.* Edited by Jerald C. Brauer. New York: Harper & Row, 1966.

IH   *The Interpretation of History.* New York: Charles Scribner's Sons, 1936.

LPJ   *Love, Power, and Justice.* New York: Oxford University Press, 1954.

MB   *Morality and Beyond.* New York: Harper & Brothers, 1963. Republished with introduction by William Schweiker. Louisville: Westminster John Knox, 1995.

MSFA   *My Search for Absolutes.* New York: Simon and Schuster, 1967.

NB   *The New Being.* New York: Charles Scribner's Sons, 1955.

OB   *On the Boundary: An Autobiographical Sketch.* New York: Charles Scribner's Sons, 1966.

PE   *Political Expectation.* Edited by James Luther Adams. New York: Harper & Row, 1971.

RS   *The Religious Situation.* New York: Meridian Books, 1956.

SD   *The Socialist Decision.* New York: Harper & Row, 1977.

SF   *The Shaking of the Foundations.* New York: Charles Scribner's Sons, 1948.

ST   *Systematic Theology.* 3 vols. Chicago: University of Chicago Press, 1951–63.

TC   *Theology of Culture.* New York: Oxford University Press, 1959.

TPE   *The Protestant Era.* Chicago: University of Chicago Press, 1948.

WIR   *What Is Religion?* Edited by James Luther Adams. New York: Harper & Row, 1969.

CHAPTER ONE

LIFE AND CAREER

James William McClendon once wrote that all theology is autobiography. That aphorism and its cognate—that all theology is contextual—surely apply to Paul Tillich's theology, which was decisively shaped by his life's personal and cultural contexts. A sketch of his life and the shape of his career illumine this intersection.

Tillich was born into a Lutheran pastor's home on August 20, 1886, in Starzeddel, Germany (now Poland). Until 1933 he resided in Germany; in that year he immigrated to the United States, where he lived the remainder of his life in New York City, Boston, and Chicago. After he died on October 25, 1965, his ashes were interred at Paul Tillich Park in New Harmony, Indiana.

Tillich studied at the universities of Berlin, Tübingen, Halle, and Breslau. Seminal influences on him were the theologian Martin Kähler, the idealist philosopher Friedrich Schelling, the religious theorist Rudolf Otto, and the existentialist philosopher Martin Heidegger. Schelling was the topic of both of his dissertations, at Breslau in 1910 and at Halle in 1912. While at Halle, he became an army chaplain during World War I. His experiences with violence and death caused him psychological trauma, resulting in treatments and expressing itself in radical shifts of his point of view. When the war ended, for example, he received an appointment at the University of Berlin, where he became a social and political activist, sharply criticizing capitalism and embracing religious socialism. His marriage to Margarethe Wever (in 1914) ended in divorce in 1921. In 1924 he married Hannah Gottschow.

Also in 1924 Tillich became a professor of theology at Marburg, where Rudolf Otto and Martin Heidegger were colleagues. In 1925 he moved to a position in Dresden, and in 1927 to the University of Leipzig. Then from 1929 to 1933 he served at the University of Frankfurt as professor of philosophy until the Nazis dismissed him from his position for his public criticism of the Hitler regime and his close relationship with Jewish intellectuals.

With the support of Reinhold Niebuhr, in 1933, he left Germany for a position at Union Theological Seminary in New York City, where he taught until 1955. Thereafter, he became University Professor at Harvard University and, in 1962, the Nuveen Professor of Divinity at The University of Chicago until his death.[1]

A prolific writer and frequent lecturer, Tillich addressed public and academic audiences with such clarity that many of his works remain in print. Foremost is his *Systematic Theology*, published in three separate volumes in 1951, 1957, and 1963. Other notable works are *The Courage to Be* (1952), *Love, Power, and Justice* (1954), and *The Dynamics of Faith* (1957). Collected essays include *The Protestant Era* (1948), *Theology of Culture* (1959), *What Is Religion?* (1969), *Political Expectation* (1971), and *The Thought of Paul Tillich* (1985). A fruitful entryway into Tillich's intellectual world is through his sermons, which are collected in *The Shaking of the Foundations* (1948), *The New Being* (1955), and *The Eternal Now* (1963). Engaging autobiographical writings include *On the Boundary* (1966), *My Search for Absolutes* (1967), and *My Travel Diary* (1970). A selection of Tillich's writings can be accessed at www.religion-online.org. Click on "Tillich." At the conclusion of this volume, there is a bibliography of primary and secondary sources.

By the mid-1950s Tillich had become the most notable and perhaps the most controversial theologian in America. In 1959 he appeared on the cover of *Time*, which featured him as America's "foremost Protestant thinker."[2] In 1963 he was the plenary speaker at the magazine's fortieth anniversary dinner, addressing hundreds of celebrities who had appeared on *Time*'s cover. Through the 1960s, he was the visible face of American theology.

Along with Karl Barth, he remains an abiding presence in theology. In a speech to the American Academy of Religion in 1989, Jonathan Z. Smith, in an analysis of the structure and ethos of the scholarly study of religion, noted that "Tillich remains the unacknowledged theoretician of our entire enterprise." Professor Smith, a historian of religion at The University of Chicago, references the expanse of the study of religion per se and not merely Christian theology.[3] Tillich's work continues to be an object of study in colleges, universities, seminaries, and divinity schools. Scholars continue to write dissertations, monographs, and articles on him, often in comparison or contrast with newer approaches to theology. The North American Paul Tillich Society supports scholarship on Tillich along with its German counterpart, the Deutsche-Paul-Tillich-Gesellschaft.

For some, like the authors of this text, Tillich is an iconic figure, a deep and serious person of faith who was a brave and creative interpreter of the core of Christian belief. For others, he is a representative of all that is wrong with theology. He is portrayed as a betrayer and denier of historic orthodoxy, a heretic, a relativist, and even an atheist. Despite the deep divide of opinion about Tillich, there is considerable veracity to Yale professor John E. Smith's aphorism: "You can think with him or against him, but not without him."[4]

In approaching Tillich's thought, a reader needs to keep several orientations in mind in order to understand his work. Central, as many interpreters have noted, he is a thinker "on the boundaries." Perhaps no other point is as important for "getting" what Tillich is saying. This application of a boundary metaphor suggests a style of thinking that mediates between "this" and "that," typically finding a concept with polar extremes in tension with each other. He speaks, for example, of being and nonbeing, the infinite and the finite, essence and existence, the human and the divine, life and death, the Catholic substance and the Protestant principle, and faith and doubt. In some sense these dualities are the opposite of each other, but at the same time, they are in lively tension with each other.

As one on the boundary between two concepts or contexts, Tillich was also "in" each of the poles of a "boundary situation." He was a person with his feet in worlds and thoughts in tension. He also lived on a variety of cultural and contextual boundaries throughout his life. His thought traversed between idealist and realist orientations. He was pointedly objective and rational but with a polar tension with nature and emotion. An objective and a romantic thinker, a philosopher and a theologian, an academic and a preacher, a European and an American, and an optimist and a pessimist—he referred to living on and in boundary situations as being on a frontier:

> Existence on the frontier, in the boundary situation, is full of tension and movement. It is in truth not standing still, but rather a crossing and return, a repetition of return and crossing, a back-and-forth—the aim of which is to create a third area beyond the bounded territories, an area where one can stand for a time without being enclosed in something tightly bounded.[5]

This dialectical rhythm will be copiously illustrated as we describe his core ideas on almost every page in this volume.

One of the many ways that this kind of thinking is manifest in his work is in his most important publication, *Systematic Theology*. In this three-volume project, he seeks to bring the poles of reason and revelation into a creative dialogue so as to find "a third area beyond the bounded territories" of philosophy and theology. In this introduction to his thought, as we work through his magnum opus, we find the rhythm of his dialectical thinking, of question and answer, on every page. To accomplish this amazing consideration of "either/or" or "both/and," he employs his famous "method of correlation." Simply put, he asks five core questions from philosophical reason and provides five answers from faithful belief. Thus, the system is divided into five sections:

1. Reason and Revelation—a study of human rationality in unity with the structures of reality; the questions about reality implied in reason; and the answers about reality proposed by faith.
2. Being and God—a study of humanity's essential nature; the questions of reason about human finitude; and the answers of faith about God.
3. Existence and Christ—the study of human existence as estrangement; the questions of reason implied in existence; and the answers of faith about Jesus as the Christ.
4. Life and the Spirit—the study of humanity as living; the questions of reason about the ambiguities of life; and the answers of faith about spiritual presence.
5. History and the Kingdom of God—an analysis of humanity's existence in history; the questions implied in the ambiguities of history; and the answers of faith with reference to the kingdom of God.

We follow this introductory overview with a chapter on Tillich's theological method and use of language (chapter 2). Then we offer a guide through these five major sections of *Systematic Theology* (chapters 3 through 7). Chapters 8 and 9 treat two of Tillich's most important contributions, those of faith and a theology of culture; and in chapter 10 we highlight the abiding import of Tillich for our time. Finally, because Tillich distinctly employed words and phrases, we have provided a lexicon of key words and phrases that are crucial to his concepts.

Questions for Reflection

1. How important are a theologian's life experiences to his or her theology? Should, for example, a divorce or a violent experience such as war or a dislocation from one culture to another be a factor in the theologian's thinking? If so, to what extent?

2. If theology has to do with the enunciation of eternal truths, what value is brought to theology from finite, human experiences?

CHAPTER TWO

METHOD AND SYMBOLS

The sources of systematic theology can be sources only for one who participates in them, that is, through experience.[1]

The object of theology is found in the symbols of religious experience.[2]

The language of faith is the language of symbols.[3]

The wholly transcendent transcends every symbol of the Holy.[4]

For Paul Tillich, theology is the enterprise of bringing the core concepts of Christianity intelligibly into our present existence. The kerygma of faith—its message—must be explained in contemporary language. The classic symbols and concepts related to God, Christ, Spirit, church, and kingdom, for example, must be expounded in contemporary language in order to be understood. Thus Tillich defines *theology* as "the methodical explanation of the contents of the Christian faith."[5] Moreover, it is an apologetic or "answering" theology because "it answers the questions implied in the 'situation' [i.e., the cultural milieu] in the power of the eternal message [i.e., the gospel kerygma] with the means provided by the situation whose questions it answers."[6]

Tillich's foremost partner in the theological task is philosophy, specifically the philosophical enterprise that raises existential questions about the structure of being. Correspondingly, he recognizes that theology also presupposes the structure of being "in every sentence." While "philosophy deals with the structure of being in itself," Tillich determines that "theology deals with the meaning of being for us."[7] Tillich concludes that all of the "big" questions of philosophy—questions about "time, space, cause, thing, subject, nature, freedom, necessity, life, value, knowledge, experience, being and not-being"—are presupposed "on every page of every religious or theological text."[8]

Because culture and philosophy pose the pertinent religious questions, Tillich reasons that the answers of theology cannot be a recital of scriptures and creedal statements but require the language of our present existence. Tillich therefore creates new ways of understanding traditional theology's symbols, such as God as being itself or Being, sin as estrangement and alienation, Christ as the New Being, and the presence of God as *kairos*. In order to grasp Tillich's theology, one must grasp these new terms. Tillich himself raises a question that some of his critics have also put forth when he asks, "Can the Christian message be adapted to the modern mind without losing its essential and unique character?"[9]

Tillich's response is the development and application of a "method of correlation" that "tries to correlate the questions implied in the situation with the answers implied in the message."[10] Embedded in and reflecting upon the human condition, his method of correlation begins with existential questions framed and posed by philosophy and culture. To these questions, then, theology must provide answers. This responsive interaction is not a presumptive theological assertion of its privilege in resolving the existential conundrums articulated by philosophy. Since philosophy and culture participate in the very ground of being that provides the ultimate goal and criterion of theology itself, the formulation of the questions emerges from religious situations. Philosophy and culture are not befuddled by these situations; instead, they provide the means—the discursive language and the linguistic symbols—for specifying and articulating the problematic situations and conditions.

For Tillich, the task of philosophy is to draw from an analysis of the human condition and its experience of finitude and then to formulate questions of ultimate significance. In response, theology must move beyond stodgy concepts that merely reiterate scriptural lessons and historic dogmatic assertions to locate answers in evocative, revelatory symbols. Tillich's method of correlation involves more than the logical application of certain criteria to central symbols of Christian tradition. Instead, his method of correlation, as Mark Kline Taylor notes, "is an interpretive art requiring sensitive readings of both human situations and also of Christian symbols in the tradition. It is a continual tacking back and forth between a situation and a Christian message that are always already in some kind of mutual interrelation."[11]

While it addresses the questions articulated by philosophy and culture, theology must also wrestle with unanticipated challenges by new philosophical propositions and cultural expressions, bracketing its anticipated answers to recurrent questions and reenvisioning responses in light of the new dimensions of the questions and situations. Yet the answers proposed by Christian theology are meaningful, Tillich avers, "only in so far as they are in correlation with questions concerning the whole of our existence, with existential questions."[12]

Tillich developed his method of correlation in a conscious attempt to avoid, as he put it, several "contradictory errors in theology"—the supranaturalistic, the naturalistic, and the dualistic. The supranaturalistic tendency, he observes, "makes revelation a rock falling into history from above, to be accepted obediently without preparation or adequacy to human nature." By contrast, the naturalistic orientation "replaces revelation by a structure of rational thought derived from and judged by human nature." Avoiding the errors engendered in both perspectives, the method of correlation "shows a way out of the blind alley in which the discussion between fundamentalism or neo-orthodoxy on the one hand, and theological humanism or liberalism on the other, is caught."[13] The third inadequate method that Tillich identifies is dualistic. In a minimal way, it recognizes and tries to address the problem that the method of correlation resolves. Building upon the naturalistic and supranaturalistic methods, the dualistic method seeks to explicate a positive relation between them "by positing a body of theological truth." Persons can reach this body of theological truth by exploring "natural revelation" (an oxymoron!), especially as it might be formulated in the so-called proofs of the "existence of God"—a phrase that Tillich also regards as self-contradictory since God is being itself and is not bound by the structures and strictures of existence.[14]

In the method of correlation, two formal criteria are central. The first is that "the object of theology is what concerns us ultimately."[15] Consequently, only the unconditioned or infinite is a proper object of theology. All other concerns are preliminary; and the elevation of a secondary or preliminary object or idea to ultimacy is idolatry, which is the bane of theology. At the same time, because all preliminary concerns are grounded in the ultimate, they can become vehicles (or symbols) that point beyond their finite existence to the ultimate. In this way, then, artistic expressions, historical events and narratives, psychological insights, social ideas and actions, legal projects and procedures, and political programs and decisions can become viable objects and valid concerns for theological exploration and reflection. The second formal criterion of theology is that which concerns us ultimately, "that which determines our being or nonbeing."[16] We belong to being, but in our existence we are separated from its fullness, which we long for. In existence, humans—and all other existents—are threatened by nonbeing and seek meaning that establishes their reunion with human essence, or being. Christian theology claims that by overcoming the brokenness of human existence, Jesus as the Christ is the principle of the possibility of reunion. In philosophical terms, Tillich posits a correlation between the ultimate and the finite— between essence and existence—based on the assumption that reality has a structure that can be known at least formally. "The power of being ... expresses itself in and through the structure of being. Therefore, we can encounter it, be grasped by it, know it, and act toward it."[17]

Although theology cannot be constrained by the language and concepts of Scripture and the creeds, Tillich does recognize their significance as sources for theology, four of which he delineates. First, the Bible—especially the Pauline Epistles— contains inspired witness of human response to revelatory events related to being. Building upon the receipt and appropriation of the biblical witness, theological developments in the life of the church—including its creeds—constitute a second source for theology. A third source involves the existential context in which the theologian appropriates the biblical witness and historical development within the church. And fourth, drawing from the existential context, the theologian must use aspects, artifacts, and expressions of one's culture "to discover the ultimate concern in the ground of a philosophy, a political system, and artistic style, a set of ethical or social principles."[18]

The "medium" through which the theologian sifts these sources of theological thought is the cultural milieu of the theologian and the theologian's personal experiences. The theologian, bound to the event of Jesus as the Christ, is "bound to the Christian message which he must derive from other sources than his experience."[19] Meanwhile, the theologian also must not exclude the cultural and personal context of one's experience and not allow the context to become dominant and distort the message. The theologian must work creatively in this interplay, invoking the norm by which all theological statements are evaluated, specifically, the New Being in Jesus as the Christ as theology's ultimate concern. For all ecclesiastical pronouncements and theological claims are subject to the norm of Jesus as the Christ. Here Tillich rejects all orthodoxies and new orthodoxies as historically and contextually conditioned and therefore subject to revision and reform. In summary, theology is the constructive task that "does not tell us what people have thought the Christian message to be in the past; rather it tries to give us an interpretation of the Christian message which is relevant to the present situation."[20]

The fourth source for Tillich's theological task, as noted above, involves the identification and interpretation of the symbolic expressions of a culture. According to him, symbols manifest the ideas of the revelation with which theology works as it unravels responses to the provocative philosophical questions of the correlative method. The "stuff" with which theologians work is a repository of symbols provided by both experience and revelation. And as we will explore more thoroughly in chapter 4, "Being and God," the very word *God* and the interpretive designation of "being itself" are, Tillich contends, symbolic of the God beyond "God" who is the source of creation, the power of redemption, and the focus of Christian theology.

In two distinct ways Tillich's understanding of and appreciation for symbols energize his entire theological enterprise. For one, he understands that language itself is symbolic and that theological discourse in particular utilizes language in ways that enlarge possibilities for understanding the world and being as such. For another, he appreciates the power of artistic styles and linguistic expressions to tap into a culture's core and represent its anxieties and hopes.

In his various discussions of the theological significance of symbols, Tillich repeatedly distinguishes symbols from signs. The designation makes sense for his concept of symbols and signification, but it counters the popular tendency to fuse the functions of signs and symbols. According to Tillich, there are several basic characteristics of symbols, most of which distinguish them from signs. Like signs, however, symbols are figurative: they point beyond themselves to a meaning that exceeds their own presentation. "This implies that something which is intrinsically invisible, ideal, or transcendent is made perceptible in the symbols and is in this way given objectivity." And Tillich continues, "The perceptibility of the symbol need not be sensuous. It can just as well be something imaginatively conceived."[21]

Unlike signs, however, symbols participate in the reality of their referents. In this way they exemplify and transmit the power of that to which they point. The referential power of symbols means that they open up levels of reality—levels of meaning and being—that in many respects would remain inexpressible and inaccessible. The power of symbols, then, enables them to open up simultaneously in two directions—toward the reality to which they refer and toward the innermost regions of selfhood. As Tillich puts it, the symbol "not only opens up dimensions and elements of reality which otherwise would remain unapproachable but also unlocks dimensions and elements of our soul which correspond to the dimensions and elements of reality."[22]

Another distinction between signs and symbols is that signs can be created for specific purposes, which means that they also can be changed at will. Because of their participatory power, symbols, unlike signs, cannot be intentionally created, arbitrarily changed, or purposefully exchanged. Symbols emerge somewhat organically out of life because "they always are results of a creative encounter with reality."[23] Even as the birth of symbols is different from that of signs, so too is their way of death or destruction, their demise into impotence. A sign, for instance, can be destroyed by an administrative decision to replace it with another sign, much like the letterhead of a corporation might be changed for self-serving purposes to reflect a shift in administrative leadership or marketing initiatives. But a symbol, Tillich contends, can die only when its germinating situation disintegrates or disappears. Even scientific criticism cannot kill symbols; it can only profane them by focusing on them as objects to be examined and celebrated in themselves rather than exploring their disclosive potential.

A fourth basic characteristic of symbols involves their public nature, cultural particularity, and social relevance. Someone, for example, can devise a sign for his or her personal use, but one cannot invent a symbol or claim to recognize a symbol for oneself alone. If something is to become a symbol, it must do so in the context of a community that can affirm and share the symbolic nature and referent of that which serves as a symbol.

The adequacy, truth, or authenticity of a symbol frequently cannot be determined by a comparison of the symbol with its referent since the symbol's referent otherwise often lies beyond the reach of human comprehension or imagination. The authenticity, adequacy, or truthfulness of a symbol, therefore, depends upon "its inner necessity for the symbol-creating consciousness"—its relative adequacy for the situation that generated it.[24]

For the most part, religious symbols function like all other symbols, which reveal hidden levels of reality—of the referent and of oneself—that otherwise would remain inaccessible. But the difference between religious symbols and all other symbols is that religious symbols refer to the other, that which is beyond the full reach of human understanding—to ultimate reality, being itself, meaning itself. Religious symbols disclose "the depth dimension of reality, the dimension of reality which is the ground of every other dimension and every other depth, and which, therefore, is not one level beside the others but is the fundamental level, the level below all other levels, the level of being itself, or the ultimate power of being."[25] Although religious symbols in some way represent an encounter with God, they do not make God immanent, for as Tillich poetically puts it, "The wholly transcendent transcends every symbol of the Holy." Since religious symbols represent that which is unconditionally beyond human comprehension, a question arises about what material might adequately express ultimate reality. Tillich himself notes that religious symbols take their material from all kinds of experiences—natural, personal, and historical—and that "everything in time and space has become at some time in the history of religion a symbol for the Holy."[26]

The problem for all symbols, but especially for religious symbols, is that they often tend to become identified completely with that which they symbolize. In so doing they have a tendency to supplant their referents. The problem is heightened by the nature of the dual task of religious symbols, which must express not only ultimate reality but also the character of the material that serves as the symbol.[27] The symbol must not be transparent, losing all its self-identity; instead, it must be translucent, maintaining its own character but revealing light from another source. When religious symbols become confused with the reality they represent, they become idolatrous and demonic, for idolatry is nothing other than making symbols of the holy absolute and identical with the holy itself. A strong example of the confusion of a symbol with that which it represents is the Bible. Its passages reveal the God beyond God whose work they identify, confront, and often celebrate. But fundamentalists confuse the symbolic, referential power of the Bible (which, like all symbols, participates in the power of that—of God—to which or to whom it refers) with the divine itself, and thereby they make the Bible an object of idolatry. In one sure sense, however, religious symbols are holy, for they do participate in the sacred character of that to which they refer. They are not holy, however, "in and of themselves, but they are holy by their participation in that which is the holy itself, the ground of all holiness."[28]

The authenticity, adequacy, and truth of religious symbols, like those of all other symbols, depend not upon the relation of the symbol to its referent because without symbols of God, we could not express the reality of the divine. "God is the basic symbol of faith, but not the only one," Tillich avers. And all of the divine attributes that we conceive, such as "power, love, justice, are taken from finite experiences and applied symbolically to that which is beyond finitude and infinity."[29]

The truth of religious symbols depends upon the adequacy of the symbols expressing the relation of a community to the revelation received by the community. Further differentiating the truth expressed by symbols, Tillich identifies degrees of truth expressed by religious symbols.

> A religious symbol possesses some truth if it adequately expresses the correlation of revelation in which some person stands. A religious symbol is true if it adequately expresses the correlation of some person with final revelation. A religious symbol can die only if the correlation of which it is an adequate expression dies. This occurs whenever the revelatory situation changes and former symbols become obsolete.[30]

Basically, then, the truth and life of religious symbols depend upon their adequacy to plumb the depth of the existential situations that generate and sustain them.

Tillich also classifies various levels of religious symbols by identifying their orientation to transcendent or immanent realms. Symbols oriented to the transcendent point directly to the holy itself. On this level symbols attempt to liberate our conception of God from traditional theistic formulations and thus to resist the identification of ultimate reality with the God of traditional theism. For example, the word *God* is a self-transcendent symbol of the God beyond the God of traditional theism and even beyond the God signified by the evocative and expansive pronouncement "God," for "that which is the true and ultimate transcends the realm of finite reality infinitely." And Tillich succinctly concludes that "religiously speaking, God transcends his own name."[31]

The immanent orientation of religious symbols is made up of two levels of objective symbolic configurations, the first of which is the sacramental level. In this category, everyday events, persons, and things can be bearers of the holy, for here the sacred is represented in time and space. The danger involved with using sacramental symbols is that a person may tend to identify them exclusively and completely with the holy, which they in fact represent. When this confusion occurs, Tillich concludes, "religion relapses into magic."[32] The second level of immanent religious symbols is the liturgical level, which includes an array of "sign-symbols," that is, things that rituals use and tradition has elevated from the realm of signs to that of symbols. Included in this level are clerical garbs and prayerful gestures, sounds (like the classic ringing of the sacring bell) and smells (like the incense offered in a consecrating rite).

Tillich reasons that because God is not a being beside other beings, because—strictly speaking—God does not exist, it is impossible "to give a conceptual explanation of

God."[33] The very nature of God as transcendent precludes the possibility of disclosing and explaining God in discursive language. Throughout history, a normative question for theology has been: How can God become the object of conceptual discourse? But knowing that God is beyond conceptual explanation, Tillich then alters the question to: "How is theology possible if God is beyond explanatory discourse?" In response, he regards the manifestations of God—the symbols of God—the object of theological discourse.

"The object of theology is found in the symbols of religious experience. They are not God, but they point to God. God may be said to be the object of theology but only indirectly. The direct object of theology is found only in religious symbols."[34] For Tillich, religious symbols lie at the heart of the theological enterprise, providing the pulse of its energy. In fact, a person's "ultimate concern must be expressed symbolically, because symbolic language alone is able to express the ultimate."[35]

In this way, Tillich conceives theology as being the exploration, explanation, and evaluation of symbols that manifest the human experience of ultimate reality. He specifies that constructive theology can be undertaken by one who participates in the experience of the holy that gives rise to the symbols with which he or she deals. The relation of the constructive theologian to the holy thus reflects the participatory power that symbols enjoy in relation to their referents.[36]

Given this view of symbols, Tillich identifies three functions of theology, the first of which is the process of exploring the range of possible meanings of symbols by discussing and disclosing the relation of symbols of God to other symbols and to the contexts out of which they arise. The second function of theology, which is explanation, does not mean that theology should attempt to offer arguments for the validity of symbols. Theology must attempt to explain religious symbols by illuminating the relation of the symbols to that which they represent. For instance, the theologian must ask such questions as, "What is the relationship between the Bible as literature and the Bible as the Word of God?"[37] Theology must also seek to explain symbols by clarifying the relation between the religious meaning of the symbols and the simple meaning of the material or word that serves as the symbol. The third function of theology— an evaluation or criticism of symbols—must be accomplished within the context of symbolic meaning, criticizing symbols from inside their referential realm, judging them from inside the community for which the symbols serve effectively, and comparing the symbolic elements to the entire symbolic structure of which they are a part.

The importance of symbols for theology is that through the interpretation of religious symbols, truth can be pursued and personal authenticity can be explored and expressed. And for Tillich, their importance for and interaction with the process of correlation is one in which philosophy and culture establish their queries by perceiving the provocative energy of symbols, by using their expressive potential, and by exploring their disclosive power.

Questions for Reflection

1. Does Tillich's notion of apologetic theology diminish the role of the Bible in his theology? If so, what are the advantages and disadvantages of this?

2. Does Tillich's use of somewhat arcane philosophical and psychological language limit his relevance in the churches where congregants are used to the words of the Word?

REASON AND THE QUEST FOR REVELATION

Reason receives revelation in ecstasy and miracles; but reason is not destroyed by revelation, just as revelation is not emptied by reason.[1]

Revelation does not dissolve the mystery [of God] into knowledge. Nor does it add anything directly to the totality of our ordinary knowledge.[2]

Following the introductory section of *Systematic Theology*, Paul Tillich immediately addresses the topic of "reason and the quest for revelation." Reason represents the philosophical questions that are asked, while revelation unveils the answers from the Christian perspective of truth and meaning in Jesus as the Christ.

One can analyze Tillich's views on reason by attending to two central concerns: his view of the process of knowing and his understanding of the grounds of knowing. In volume 1 of *Systematic Theology*, Tillich discusses the process of knowing under the heading "The Structure of Reason," and he evaluates the grounds of knowing under the topic "Truth and Verification."

He believes theology must always "give an account of its paths to knowledge,"[3] beginning by distinguishing two concepts of reason. He identifies the ontological with the classical tradition, and he relates the technical to British empiricism. He defines ontological reason as "the structure of the mind which enables it to grasp and to shape reality."[4] In other words, he means that the knower (the structure of the mind) and the known (reality) are similarly structured (the *logos* structure). Although explanations of this mutual *logos* structure have varied in history (realism, idealism, dualism, and monism), Tillich claims that one must assume the fact of some structure, some relation, between knower and known, else knowledge would be an impossibility.

Within the structure of ontological reason he distinguishes subjective and objective reason. He closely aligns the definition of subjective reason with that of its context, ontological reason. Subjective reason "is the structure of the mind which enables it to grasp and shape reality on the basis of a corresponding structure of reality."[5] Objective reason "is the rational structure of reality which the mind can grasp and according to which it can shape reality."[6] This claim is crucial for Tillich's approach to theology that correlates essence and existence. It makes the potential of human knowledge compatible with the structures of reality.

Ontological reason has two functions: it grasps and shapes reality. "Grasping" refers to the mind's engaged "receiving" what is given in the knowing process. "Shaping" refers to the mind's active reaction to what is received. The interplay of grasping and shaping is ongoing. "In every act of reasonable reception an act of shaping is involved, and in every act of reasonable reaction an act of grasping is involved."[7]

Grasping and shaping, then, are rational acts of ontological reason. In their rational activities one can discern a basic polarity between them because of the presence of an emotional element. In receiving, a polarity exists between the cognitive and aesthetic elements. In grasping, a polarity exists between organizational and organic elements. The element of the emotional or the personal is a part of every rational act, although with varying degrees of importance in different disciplines. In music, for instance, the aesthetic element far outweighs the cognitive, while in chemistry the opposite obtains. Further, personal relationships emphasize the organic element, while relations between nations emphasize the organizational element.[8] All ways of knowing, therefore, operate on a continuum from most objective to most subjective. Later he calls this position "belief-ful realism," which also enjoys considerable status among epistemologists today.

Tillich claims that the introduction of an emotional element into the receiving and reacting functions of the knower does not make the knowing process less rational or utterly subjective. Each avenue of inquiry has its own rational structure that opens various dimensions of reality. In the language of ontological polarities, "reason unites a dynamic with a static element in an indissoluble amalgam."[9]

Tillich next introduces the idea of "depth" with regard to ontological reason. The depth of reason "is the expression of something that is not reason but which precedes reason and is manifest through it."[10] It is the ground of reason, that from which reason proceeds. The depth of reason is present in all realms of inquiry.

> In the cognitive realm the depth of reason is its quality of pointing to truth-itself, namely, to the infinite power of being and of the ultimately real, through the relative truths in every field of knowledge. In the aesthetic realm the depth of reason is its quality of pointing to "beauty-itself," namely, to an infinite meaning and an ultimate significance, through the creations in every field of aesthetic intuition. In the legal realm the depth of reason is its quality of pointing to "justice-itself," namely, to an infinite seriousness and an ultimate dignity, through every structure of actualized justice. In the communal realm the depth of reason is its quality of pointing to "love-itself," namely, to an infinite richness and an ultimate unity, through every form of actualized love. This dimension of reason, the dimension of depth, is an essential quality of all rational functions.[11]

Tillich distinguishes between essential reality, which is ontological reason, and existential reality, which is reason in concrete existence. At times he uses the terms *actual reason* or *finite reason* interchangeably with existential reason. Under the conditions of existence, a conflict emerges because the transparency of essential reason toward its depth becomes opaque due to the fact that reason in existence is reason in conflict with itself. Finite reason is therefore contradictory, ambiguous, and threatened by disruption and self-destruction.[12] He describes the conflict within actual reason in three ways: as the conflict between autonomy and heteronomy, as the conflict between relativism and absolutism, and as the conflict between formalism and emotionalism. One can chart these conflicts summarily:

1. The polarity of structure and depth produces a conflict between autonomous and heteronomous reason that results in a quest for theonomy.
2. The polarity of the static and dynamic produces a conflict between absolutism and relativism that results in a quest for the concrete-absolute.
3. The polarity of the formal and emotional produces a conflict between formalism and irrationalism that results in a quest for the union of form and mystery.

These conflicts provide the context in which reason is actualized. In the first conflict—that between autonomy and heteronomy—reason "affirms and actualizes its structure without regarding its depth as autonomous."[13] Reason that claims to express the depth of reason, but doing so on the basis of a power outside of reason, is heteronomous. Heteronomous reason emerges as a reaction against autonomous reason that has lost its depth. An autonomy that has given birth to a heteronomy results in the conflict of reason divided against itself. This conflict of reason separated within itself generates a quest for a reunion of the polarity of its structure and depth—a quest, as Tillich puts it, for a theonomy or autonomous reason reunited with its own depth.[14]

Likewise, in the conflict between absolutism and relativism, reason that actualizes the static element without regarding the dynamic element establishes two forms of absolutism. In one form, the absolutism of tradition, "the static side of reason [is defended] against an exclusive emphasis on the dynamic side." In the other form, the absolutism of revolution, the "dynamic structures of reason [are seen] as static and elevate[d] . . . to absolute validity." However, reason that denies the static element and emphasizes the dynamic element creates two forms of relativism. The first form, positivistic relativism, "takes what is 'given' [posited] without applying absolute criteria to its valuation." The other form, cynical relativism, "is disbelief in the validity of any rational act" that results in a "vacuum into which new absolutisms pour."[15]

Tillich explicates the third conflict in finite reason—that between formalism and irrationalism—in a similar manner. "Formalism appears in the exclusive emphasis on the formal side" of reason to the denial of the emotional.[16] In formalism, then, reason is reduced to strict, technically correct thinking processes. Irrationalism, however, is a reaction against formalism from solely emotional reason. Still reason, it is blind and fanatical.

Emerging from these three conflicts in actual reason is a drive toward existential reason, which is estranged from its ground and yearns to return to it. Existential reason quests for revelation or "the manifestation of the ground of being for human knowledge."[17] Tillich here correlates reason and revelation, which provides an occasion for him to distinguish the roles of philosophy and theology.

Tillich also delineates ontological reason in terms of the more familiar language of subject and object, or knower and known. He asserts that "knowledge is based on an original unity which involves a separation and a reunion of subject and object."[18] There are an original unity, necessary separation, and possible reunion. The ontological problem of knowledge is the unity of the knower's separation from the known and the knower's participation with the known. By this strange-sounding paradox, Tillich means that the knower must be detached from the object—that the knower is separated and estranged from the object of inquiry.[19] Still, knower and known are united in the way that objects of inquiry contain "essential structures with which the cognitive [knower] is essentially united."[20] In existence, knowing is the quest that "unites the certainty of existential union with the openness of cognitive detachment."[21]

The process of knowing therefore contains two fundamental elements of union and detachment. All cognitive reason contains both elements in different proportions. In "controlling knowledge," which is associated with the sciences, the knower remains primarily detached from the subject and objectifies it. "Receiving knowledge," which is associated with the humanities (including religion and theology), "takes the object into itself."[22] The aim of controlling knowledge is to exercise control, whereas the aim of receiving knowledge is to understand. Still, "there is no knowledge without the presence of both elements."[23] Cognitive distortion occurs when one disregards the polarity of union and detachment by focusing on either.

The most typical distortion deals with technical reason, which is reason "reduced to the capacity for reasoning."[24] It eliminates the emotional element from the reasoning process and with it, the polarities present in grasping and shaping. It denies the aesthetic and organic sides of the polarities. Technical reason allows for no emotive, personal, or subjective elements. As a result, it reduces the objects of its knowing to things. Tillich observes that technical reason is a legitimate element or companion of ontological reason. It has a tendency, however, to separate itself from ontological reason, although technical reason is a tool of ontological reason.[25]

Our discussion of Tillich's view of reason has thus far set out his analysis of how knowledge is possible within the structures and contours of the human mind. In epistemological terms one can describe this as the structure of the logic or context of discovery. The other major epistemological issue with which philosophers deal is the context or logic of justification. That notion seeks to specify criteria by which one measures the validity of a knowledge claim.

Tillich briefly considers this topic in *Systematic Theology* 1 under the heading "Truth and Verification." He asserts that every cognitive act strives for the truth, which has to do with the essence of things, that which gives them the power of being. "Truth," he claims, "is the essence of things as well as the cognitive act in which their essence is grasped.... A judgment is true because it grasps and expresses true being; and the really real becomes truth if it is grasped and expressed in a true judgment."[26]

But how does one judge whether a judgment is true or false, especially when all claims of absolute truth are suspect? "Every cognitive assumption [hypothesis] must be tested."[27] According to Tillich, two methods of verification correspond to the two cognitive attitudes, the controlling and the receiving. One verifies controlling knowledge by repeatable experiments; one verifies receiving knowledge by experience in the creative union of two natures. The proper objects of controlling knowledge are machines, things, and separable elements of life processes that are, however, the objects of receiving knowledge. As one would expect, controlling knowledge is relatively certain; receiving knowledge, by contrast, is necessarily indefinite, preliminary, and imprecise. Tillich observes that "controlling knowledge is safe but not ultimately significant, while receiving knowledge can be ultimately significant, but it cannot give certainty."[28]

Before discussing Tillich's correlation of reason with revelation, let us turn attention to three reflective points that may help provide perspective on his view of reason. First, Tillich's position rejects static views of reality, choosing rather to see reality—or being—as dynamic in contrast to a perspective that makes being static under the conditions of existence frequently alleged. The Parmenidean "isness" of being is a polar, Heraclitean "becoming." There is a "given" that makes the world of becoming possible. "Being is the basic absolute."[29] In existence reason evidences a polar structure, and the dynamic structure of being in existence is connected to Tillich's concept of life, spirit, and history.

Second, because ontology and epistemology have similar structures, it is no surprise that, like being, knowing is dynamic. Even as ontology is dynamic, so too Tillich's epistemology accounts for changes and shifts in what one claims as true. He affirms the relativity of all truth claims. While his ontology includes a dynamic side, so also does his epistemology. To be sure, Tillich's notion of the depth of reason clearly implies an absolute. He defines truth in terms of reason's ability to grasp the depth of an object. There are absolutes. Yet "each of our statements about the absolutes in knowledge is relative" because in existence the transparency of essential reason toward its depth is opaque and ambiguous.[30] All knowledge claims are bound to finite space and time. They are relative to the conditions of a particular existence. Nevertheless, this degree of relativity does not imply a relativism that is devoid of an absolute. Tillich holds that complete relativism is logically incoherent and practically impossible. For instance, the term *absolute relativism* is self-contradictory; yet life demands decision. Practically one lives "as though" something is true. Tillich's dialectical view of the structure of reason therefore denies the possibility of absolute knowledge; it maintains, however, the necessity of the concept of an absolute ground. Thus, Tillich rejects both thoroughgoing relativism and dogmatic absolutism.[31]

Third, Tillich includes an existential or experiential element in the knowing process. For Tillich the test of experience is the chief criterion by which one judges the validity of receiving knowledge, although experience is never completely eliminated from controlling knowledge. He elaborates the role of experience in knowing in terms of the concept of *participation*, which suggests identity between knower and known within a polarity of individualization and participation. "Subject and object meet in the situation and knowledge."[32] All understanding depends upon participation. But how does empathetic participation avoid wishful thinking or romantic idealization? Here Tillich appeals to "right" participation, meaning that true knowledge depends upon being "detached and involved at the same time."[33] In the final analysis the acknowledgment of experience or participation as an ingredient in knowing means that one cannot exactly specify the criteria of truth. Can the subject, however, be eliminated from the process? No. This insight is one of the chief accomplishments of the recent history and philosophy of science. Tillich's emphasis on participation would lead him to be receptive toward this conclusion of historically sensitive epistemologies.

While reason treats how one acquires knowledge and formulates questions, revelation is the manifestation of what concerns us ultimately. Characterized by mystery, ecstasy, and miracle, theological utterances are concrete statements of "a special and extraordinary manifestation which removes the veil from something which is hidden in a special and extraordinary way."[34] Such an event is "shaky, transforming, and demanding."[35]

As mystery, revelation discloses something experientially and cognitively. In other words, the mysterious object is experienced, and the experience becomes an object of rational expression.[36] Thus, revelations contain both subjective and objective elements. Subjectively, one is "grasped by the manifestation of the mystery." That an expression occurs is the objective side. Revelation is both given (objective) and received (subjective).[37]

When the mystery of the ultimate is manifested, ecstasy ensues. Ecstasy "is the state of the mind in which reason is beyond itself, that is, beyond its subject-object structure."[38] Even so, ecstasy is not irrational; it is neither mere enthusiasm nor a form of psychological excitement.[39] It is, rather, an "ontological shock."[40] At this point Tillich references Rudolf Otto's famous description of the human encounter of the sacred when he writes:

> In revelation and in the ecstatic experience in which it is received, the ontological shock is preserved and overcome at the same time. It is preserved in the annihilating power of the divine presence (*mysterium tremendum*) and is overcome in the elevating power of the divine presence (*mysterium fascinosum*). Ecstasy unites the experience of the abyss to which reason in all its functions is driven with the experience of the ground in which reason is grasped by the mystery of its own depth and of the depth of being generally.[41]

In addition to mystery and ecstasy, the third element in revelation is miracle. Miracle is "the sign-event which gives the mystery of revelation [and] does not destroy the rational structure of the reality in which it appears."[42]

Because everything participates in the ground of being and meaning, media of revelation can be any person, thing, community, historical event, or natural phenomenon that exists.[43] Moreover, all elements of human existence and language (the Word through words) can be agents of revelation.[44] Although words can disclose truth, there is no sacred language per se. Nor are there revealed doctrines. Language, doctrines, texts, and creeds are symbolic expressions of the mystery, ecstasy, and miracles of religious experiences.[45] Indeed, locating revelation in any finite person, object, or event is idolatrous. The media of revelation are vehicles for the message.[46] Not surprisingly, then, language about God is never literal or plain. It is analogous and symbolic. Further, because Christian theology is based on the claim that Jesus as the Christ is the decisive revelation of God, Jesus as the Christ is the criterion by which all theological claims are measured because Jesus as the Christ "becomes completely transparent to the mystery he reveals."[47] Simply, Christ is the unsurpassing medium of revelation.

After distinguishing between original and dependent revelation, Tillich discusses the actual revelation of God in Jesus as the Christ, which is, for Christianity, the final revelation. By "final revelation," Tillich means "the decisive, fulfilling, unsurpassable revelation, that which is the criterion of all others." Jesus as the Christ is the final revelation because "he becomes completely transparent to the mystery he reveals," namely, the reuniting power of being.[48] He embodies this power by negating himself, sacrificing himself completely and thus becoming the medium of essential being. According to Tillich, Jesus of Nazareth made no claims that he himself was divine or a perfect being or the knower of all truth. Had he done so, he would have avoided the sacrifice of himself and claimed powers, stature, and significance that would have made him an idol. "The claim of anything finite to be final," states Tillich, "is demonic."[49] The continuous self-surrender of Jesus enabled him to become the Christ, the decisive medium of revelation.

The New Testament picture of Jesus as the Christ portrays two characteristics necessary for a finite being to become a medium of the infinite, namely, "his maintenance of unity with God and his sacrifice of everything he could have gained for himself from this unity."[50] To be clear, Tillich specifies that the abiding presence of God in him made him Christ and not a perfection of moral, intellectual, or emotional qualities. His word, deeds, and sufferings are consequences of his unity with God, expressions of the New Being that resides within him.[51]

After treating the history of revelation (the universal manifestations of the period before the Christ, the period of preparation, and the final revelation in Jesus as the Christ),[52] Tillich identifies the spiritual community of the church that receives, interprets, and actualizes revelation with the final revelation.[53]

In the closing sections of "Reason and the Quest for Revelation," Tillich brings the two concepts into dialogue. Revelation answers the question of reason. In revelation the whole person is involved; every aspect of one's unity participates in reunion with its ground. Revelation cannot be reduced to reason alone (the intellectual distortion of faith as cognitive), to mystical experience alone (the emotional distortion of faith as mere feeling), or to ethical action (the moral distortion of faith as mere doing). Revelation rather fulfills reason, allowing reason to overcome the conflict within it between absolutism and relativism by the conquering power of love and in the ecstatic language of paradox.[54] With this foundation, Tillich then approaches the question of existence and its answer in Christ as the New Being.

Questions for Reflection

1. If theology contends to render transcendent and ultimate truth and value, how is it possible that mere humans are capable of being mediators of the ultimate and absolute? How can fallible humans be vehicles of the absolute?

2. Does Tillich's denial of the unchanging nature of theological affirmations diminish theological claims to mere opinions?

3. What are the advantages of segregating theological claims from scientific and historical assertions? What are the disadvantages?

CHAPTER FOUR

BEING AND GOD

God is nearer to us than [we are] to ourselves.[1]

To say anything about God in the literal sense of the words used means to say something false about him.[2]

The idea of God has, by misuse through objectification, lost its symbolic power in such measure that it serves largely as a concealment of the unconditioned transcendent rather than as a symbol for it.[3]

According to Paul Tillich, the fundamental question of theology is the question of God. His doctrine of God serves as the hub of his entire theological system. Even "the question of God," as he puts it, "is possible because an awareness of God is present in the question of God."[4] For Tillich, an intuitive awareness of God is instilled within every person because existence itself is possible only through the power of being, which he identifies with God.

The realization of human finitude forces every person to come to grips with this inherent awareness because "the question of God must be asked because the threat of non-being, which man experiences as anxiety, drives him to the question of being conquering non-being and courage conquering anxiety."[5] In this way Tillich shows that a person can raise the question of God without using God-talk or traditional religious language and that, therefore, one can express concern about God without even thinking that one is doing so.

Even though the question of God is a facet of the human condition, the answer to the question precedes the formulation of the question itself, for "'God' is the answer to the question implied in man's finitude; he is the name for that which concerns man ultimately."[6] Because all that exists is grounded in and sustained by God, all initiative for what is commonly called the divine-human encounter actually originates in God.[7] On their own, then, persons cannot arrive at knowledge of God or even at a symbolic apprehension of God. The awareness of God is innate in human experience because by existing, a person participates in being, which is the power of God.

As Tillich moves from the identification of the God question to consider the character of God, he examines the phenomenology of the concept of ultimacy and its grounding in human experience: "whatever concerns a man ultimately becomes a god for him, and, conversely . . . a man can be concerned ultimately only about that which is god for him."[8] Ultimate or unconditional concern categorically exceeds all preliminary and concrete concerns. In fact, the human predicament arises out of the continuous tension created by the human longing for ultimacy while living in concreteness. There can be only one concern to which ultimate allegiance is given because an ultimate concern demands a person's unconditional allegiance.

Tillich's assertion that God is "that" which ultimately concerns us is his philosophical way of conceptualizing radical monotheism and embracing the first commandment:

"You shall love the Lord your God with all your heart, and with all your soul, and with all your mind" (Matt. 22:37). Yet one's ultimate concern transcends subjective valuation. "Ultimacy stands against everything which can be derived from mere subjectivity, nor can the unconditional be found within the entire catalogue of finite objects which are conditioned by each other."[9]

However, the philosophical depiction of God as unconditioned and ultimate might make God seem impersonal, in some way a philosophical concept rather than a living power. As he identifies God as being itself, Tillich does not use the term in the abstract sense of nominalists or in a static sense like some Platonists. Instead, he associates the phrase "being-itself" as "the power of Being in everything that is, in everything that participates in Being."[10] For Tillich, then, God is fully personal (and more) because such an understanding of God is grounded in being itself, the power from which all persons come. In that sense, "God is nearer to us than [we are] to ourselves."[11]

One of the most frequent critiques of Tillich's depiction of God as being itself—even as related, living, and creative—is that it seems impersonal.[12] Yet Tillich affirms that "the symbol 'personal God' is absolutely fundamental because an existential relation is a person-to-person relation. Man cannot be ultimately concerned about anything that is less than the personal." Nevertheless, "God cannot be called a self, because the concept of 'self' implies separation from and contrast to everything which is not self."[13] In contrast to Tillich, however, theists often affirm a living God by suggesting that "personal" and "living" are nonsymbolic concepts. In no way does Tillich seek to depersonalize God, even while vigorously opposing efforts to conceive God as a person. Even though "God is called a person," Tillich asserts, God "is a person not in finite separation but in absolute and unconditioned participation in everything."[14] *Being* is greater than the personal. Being is "the ground of the personal,"[15] possessing "the ontological power of personality."[16] Simply, Being transcends the personal.[17]

In a comprehensive discussion of the being and character of God that concludes the first volume of his *Systematic Theology*, Tillich employs and analyzes three basic symbolic statements about God, each of which builds upon an understanding that God is personal: God is *living*; God is *creative*; and God is *related*. Under the rubric "God as related," Tillich considers God as holy (unapproachable), almighty (omnipotent), love, lord, and father. Under that symbol, Tillich also discusses the providence and omniscience of God, especially as "omniscience" refers to the human inability to escape responsibility and as "providence" is recognized as divine activity, not simply a divine plan.[18]

Although Tillich qualifies the meaning of the personal character of the symbols of God as living, creative, and related, he prefers to use ontological concepts and images as he discusses the reality of God. For Tillich, Being includes the process of becoming, a process that raises the question of life itself. According to Tillich, "Life is the process in which potential being becomes actual being. It is the actualization of the structural elements of being in their unity and in their tension."[19] Therefore, living, as process philosopher Charles Hartshorne puts it, "'transcends' mere actuality or mere potentiality since every actual process is *both* the potentiality of further process and the actualization of potentialities in previous process."[20]

To speak of God as living is to speak symbolically, for to speak of God as literally living would reduce God to the realm of existence, and it would deny the identity of potentiality and actuality within God. The nature of life is the process of actualization; potential becomes actual existence. Literally, then, God does not live, but God participates in life since "God participates in everything that is."[21] Even while God empowers all that lives, God is not restricted to living—to life—because God is not bound by the existents in whom and through whom God participates.

Especially in the initial responses to Tillich's first volume of the *Systematic Theology* in 1951, a number of theologians and philosophers criticized his concept of God by misconceiving Tillich's use of the term "being-itself" and the auxiliary phrases "ground of being" and "power of being." They asserted that the phrases are meaningless, devoid of cognitive content, or lacking recognizable referential meaning.[22] Frequently in his sermons Tillich referred to God as the "ground of being" or "power of being." On those occasions in particular, Tillich sought to emphasize the depth of being that underlies all that exists and the dynamic energy of being that infuses existence.

> The name of this infinite and inexhaustible depth and ground of all being is *God*. That depth is what the word *God* means. And if that word has no meaning for you, translate it, and speak of the depths of your life, of the source of your being, of your ultimate concern, of what you take seriously without any reservation. Perhaps, in order to do so, you must forget everything traditional that you have learned about God, perhaps even that word itself. For if you know that God means depth, you know much about God.[23]

"Ground," "power," and "depth" must be understood metaphorically; but their symbolic significance—which calls forth a sense of solidity, creativity, and energy—cannot be communicated fully by these referential images and concepts. For symbols have a surplus of meaning, expressing a depth of inexhaustible references that cannot be fathomed effectively in any other way. Tillich explains that symbolic language "surpasses in quality and strength the power of any non-symbolic language. One should never say 'only a symbol,' but one should say 'not less than a symbol.'"[24] The metaphors of "ground" and "depth" provide Tillich with language that resonates with his ontological concept of God, and to a certain extent these metaphors correspond to the kind of meaning identified by traditional metaphors of transcendence related to God.

Even while Tillich's concept of God as being itself has been called imprecise and impersonal, both pluralistic and atheistic perceptions challenge the idea of ultimacy. Some critics have attacked Tillich's insistence that a person's ultimate concern can be only "that" upon which one unconditionally depends by contending that a person does not have to hold or pursue a supreme goal, a unique concern, or a highest value. Some philosophers and polytheists, for example, claim that a person can have numerous equivalent primary concerns, none of which will ever exert the power and prominence of ultimacy.[25] However, a person could exist with numerous (seemingly equal) preliminary concerns without experiencing or designating one of them as ultimate (in a sense other than merely as a "last resort"); the person's apparent ultimate concern would seem to be his or her freedom of not having to decide between primary concerns. In fact, Tillich declares that absolute "indifference toward the ultimate question is the only imaginable form of atheism."[26]

It is possible, of course, that someone could elevate a secondary concern to a position of supposed ultimacy. But such a misappropriation would be idolatrous since ultimate concern is fundamentally associated with the quality of the holy. For, Tillich reasons, "only that which is holy can give man ultimate concern, and only that which gives man ultimate concern has the quality of holiness."[27] Everything is related to the holy, which can be manifest in and through the secular and finite because everything draws its very existence from God, from being itself. In addition, Tillich says, "everything secular is also potentially sacred, open to consecration."[28] Frequently, the ultimate can be seen through the finite objects and perceived in temporal concepts, all of which owe their existence to the power of being and thus can serve as symbols for the ultimate. Symbols, then, are the media for revelation.

Traditional images and language of God represent the divine as supreme ruler of the universe, history, and nature, and as a benevolent but disciplining parent—the familiar "Abba" or "Papa," as Jesus suggested. In one sermon, however, Tillich claims that "those are not pictures of God, but rather of man, trying to make God in his own image and for his own comfort."[29] Even so, traditional symbols of God have become brittle, often being taken for nearly literal expressions about the character or reality of God. "The idea of God has, by misuse through objectification, lost its symbolic power in such measure that it serves largely as a concealment of the unconditioned transcendent rather than as a symbol for it."[30]

One of Tillich's most provocative contributions to philosophical theology is his recognition that God does not exist. If humans try to think about God as existing, they make God an object beside other objects, actually expressing idolatry rather than affirming the divine. Even when attempts are made to underscore the greatness of God by using superlatives such as *greatest*, *most merciful*, and *most powerful*, the very use of superlatives reduces the majesty and power of God because they bring the concept of God into a spectrum of comparison with others. Instead, Tillich insists, God is *beyond* superlatives. God is categorically different rather than being fully superior in comparative ways. Being itself exceeds, yet includes, the exemplars of spatiality, substantiality, and temporality.

When one begins to consider the possibility that God exists rather than that God *is* the one revealed to Moses as Yahweh, as "I am who I am," as being itself, one begins the process of denying the reality of God. For "the first step to atheism is always a theology which drags down God to the level of doubtful things."[31] Because God is being itself, not *a* being, Tillich contends that it is as atheistic to profess the existence of God as it is to deny God's existence. For existence characterizes things and ideas, bound by the limits of finitude: substance, space, and time. As being itself, however, God transcends the categories and specificities of substance, space, and time. The only meaningful way, then, to talk about the existence of God is to talk about the existence of God incarnate, as New Being perceived fully in the historic revelation of God in Jesus as the Christ. Simply, although God does not exist, God is beyond essence and existence. Not only does being itself transcend and include everything that exists, being itself also transcends and includes infinity.[32]

Traditional arguments for the existence of God actually deny the reality of God because the concept of existence is confining and because the process of arguing the reality of God demeans the grandeur of God.[33] If God could be defined by the conclusion of an argument, then God would be reduced to the same categorical level as the other elements of the argument. Still, arguments for the existence of God function in a positive way because they show the seriousness of human concern about knowing God.

Although Tillich initially claimed that the designation "being-itself" is the only nonsymbolic statement that one can make about God,[34] he came to recognize that even that phrase and the designation of Being (with uppercase B to identify the reality, majesty, and potency of being itself) had symbolic character. The very use of language, which is a symbol system, requires that all of its semantics be referential, thus symbolic. And second, appreciating the truly awesome, majestic, and transcendent character of the holy requires recognition that language itself, however denotative in its reference, is not the transcendent itself. God transcends even the philosophical references of phrases and names attempting to signify God. Tillich states, "If we make *one* non-symbolic assertion about God, [the] ecstatic-transcendent character seems to be challenged."[35] Or again, he asserts that the word *God* is a symbol for God because God transcends even the name itself. "This is why," Tillich notes, "the use of his name easily becomes a blasphemy."[36]

Consequently, following his completion of the first volume of his *Systematic Theology*, wherein he writes extensively about the reality of God, Tillich recognized the limitations of his earlier assertions that "being-itself is the only non-symbolic statement that can be made about God." In the opening pages of the second volume, therefore, he writes, "*Everything* we say about God is symbolic. Such a statement is an assertion about God which is itself not symbolic. Otherwise we would fall into a circular argument."[37] And he expounds, when we use the language of the "infinite," and "being-itself" in reference to God, he explains, "we speak rationally and ecstatically at the same time. These terms precisely designate the boundary line at which both the symbolic and the non-symbolic coincide."[38] Holding the designation "being-itself" on the boundary between the symbolic and the nonsymbolic, Tillich maintains that "being-itself" is the most nearly pure of all symbolic statements about God. But because symbolic language "surpasses in quality and strength the power of any non-symbolic language[,] one should never say 'only a symbol,' but one should say 'not less than a symbol.'"[39]

Personal relationship with God is the goal of redemption in overcoming the alienation that characterizes the fundamental human condition (finitude, which separates persons from the fullness of being itself), yet God should not be conceived as person. To conceive God as the perfect person would abnegate the uniqueness and power of the incarnation, wherein being itself was revealed fully and afresh as New Being. As Tillich notes about personal designations related to God, "God cannot be called a self, because the concept of 'self' implies separation from and contrast to everything which is not self."[40]

In the concluding sections of the first volume of his *Systematic Theology*, Tillich introduces the symbol of Spirit to describe the living character of Being. He understands that Spirit is not a power contrasted to the material dimensions of bodily existence; instead he thinks of Spirit as embracing all existence, all elements or facets of being itself: "That God is Spirit means that life as spirit is the inclusive symbol for divine life."[41]

In connection with the consideration of God as Spirit, Tillich examines the concepts about the Trinity. "God's life," he writes, "is life as spirit and the Trinitarian principles are moments within the divine process of the divine life."[42] For Tillich, the Trinity is not a mathematical conundrum of affirming Three in One and One in Three. He perceives confusion in discussing one symbol (person) within the context of another symbol (Trinity), and so he discusses the "three-ness" of the Trinity in qualitative terms, focusing on principles rather than on quantitative terms. The first principle is "that which makes God God..., the inexhaustible ground of being in which everything has its origin." The second principle—*logos*—"unites meaningful structure and creativity," and the third principle is, of course, the Spirit, which actualizes and unifies the first two principles. "God as Spirit is the ultimate unity of both power and meaning."[43] That is, God as Spiritual Presence unites the power of being and the power of reconciliation.

The living character of Being is also identified with love, for "God is love. And, since God is being-itself, one must say that being-itself is love. This, however, is understandable only because the actuality of being is life. The process of the divine life has the character of love."[44]

The symbol of creativity also discloses who God is. God's creativity is dynamic: God created the world, God creatively sustains the world, and God will work creatively to fulfill the destiny of the world as the kingdom of God.

Tillich's ontological concept of God is not, however, a pantheistic formulation that God is all that is. Instead, Tillich's concept of God is panentheistic: God is the one in whom we live and move and have our being. God includes all that exists, all events and relationships that have transpired to form history, and all possibilities that comprise the future. And beyond that describable magnitude of God, there is more to God—the "God beyond God," as Tillich put it in *The Courage to Be*.

Questions for Reflection

1. Is it possible for a theologian to deny the existence of the God of theism and remain a Christian theologian? If so, what is lost and gained by such a denial?
2. To what extent is atheism a religious position?
3. Does Tillich adequately avoid the common charge of pantheism?

EXISTENCE AND NEW BEING

The power of essential being is ambiguously present in all existential distortions.[1]
Existence is rooted both in ethical freedom and in tragic destiny.[2]

Christianity is the message of the New Creation, the New Being, the New Reality
which has appeared with the appearance of Jesus who for this reason, and just for
this reason, is called the Christ.[3]

Throughout his volumes of sermons, existential essays in *The Courage to Be* and *Love, Power, and Justice,* and several of his philosophically oriented works such as *The Interpretation of History,* Paul Tillich frequently references ideas related to the human hopes for and experiences of New Being. In keeping with this philosophical orientation, which orients the first volume of *Systematic Theology,* Tillich develops his Christology in the second volume of *Systematic Theology.* Even as the foundational ontological question—"Why is there something rather than nothing?"—drives one to consider the uniqueness of being itself, or God, so too the condition of existence—its ambiguous, finite, and disunited character—prompts questions about the human condition. The New Being, or the Christ, is the locus of theological answers.

Tillich's Christology is closely tied to his concept of God, which provides the foundation of theological thinking, which, Tillich reasons, lies in the relationship between being—or essence, as it was classically formulated by Plato—and existence. He adapts Plato's understanding of "form" or "idea," identifying it as essence or that which underlies, energizes, and defines the ideal of all that exists. Since essence in this sense is the pure, intended form of all that exists, it is the criterion against which all existents are then measured.

The context for Tillich's Christology is the human predicament of existence itself, which he analyzes in terms of its temporality and its imperfect realization of the fullness of being itself. For Tillich, the intention of creation was a unified relationship between God and the created order, and yet by virtue of the actualization of creation, its estrangement—its pervasive and permanent separation—occurred. The symbolic story of the fall, therefore, relates the way in which the actuality of existence for humans has become the human predicament. In short, the fall resulted from the actualization of human freedom, which is a constituent component of human existence. Still, arising out of the fall is the human pursuit for New Being—the fulfillment of creation, the restoration of the intended, unbroken relationship with being itself. The very fact that humans anticipate and search for New Being means that they sense that they have "lost" something, some phase of innocence or some intended perfection. The very fact that humans continue to pursue an answer to their plight means that all traces of their original intent have not been obliterated. Addressing this flawed condition of human memory and anxiety, of human inadequacy and failure, the New

Being revealed in Jesus as the Christ provides assurance of the human quest for the restoration of persons with being itself.

Like other Christian theologians, Tillich identifies the fall as precipitating the need for human salvation through the revelation of the Christ—the appearance of New Being. But unlike many biblical theologians, even those who understand the narratives of Edenic transgression and expulsion as myth, Tillich identifies the fall with creation itself, with the temporal and spatial constrictions that separate all existents from being itself. The identification of the fall with creation means that the fall is ontological rather than historical; it precedes time, for the creation of time itself is part of the fall, the separation of existents from the eternality of being itself. In this sense, then, Tillich is able to affirm that "the Fall is not a break, but an imperfect fulfillment" of intended creation.[4]

Even locating the fall in prehistoric action, Tillich does not discount the meaningfulness of the Edenic narrative as an account of a fall from purity. For by its symbolic power as "dreaming innocence," essential being provides the standard against which all existents are measured. The story of the temptation of Adam and Eve identifies how that state of dreaming innocence is subjected to temptation; and with the exercise of freedom, which is ontologically a part of creation, the fall occurs. For Tillich, the fall is not an inevitable consequence of freedom; it is a constitutive part of freedom and a fact of existence.

Although it would seem that creation itself would thus be tainted by evil, Tillich insists that the created order is good in its essential being, but that in its actualized state, creation is estranged from its essence. This condition of estrangement, which is Tillich's understanding of sin, necessitates reconciliation and prompts the human quest for reunion with being itself. "Original or hereditary sin," he writes, "is neither original nor hereditary; it is the universal destiny of estrangement which concerns every man."[5] This state of being in sin does not minimize the responsibility that humans exercise for their own sinful acts, their willful rebuffing of God that leads them to self-glorification. In turn, expressions of pride generate a drive for complete control of one's relations, a desire that Tillich recognizes as "concupiscence." Here, following Augustine, Tillich presses beyond the common association of concupiscence with the erotic to locate it in the deepest level of human experience, in the very structure of reality.

Even as Tillich conceives the fall and sin as ontological facts, so too does he regard death as an ontological necessity. Unlike the classic Christian belief that death is the consequence of sin, Tillich understands that death is a part of existence, that it establishes a limit of temporal finitude. Nonetheless, Tillich connects death with sin, as does Paul in 1 Corinthians 15:56, noting that sin provides "the sting of death," which is the anxiety that grows out of estrangement by recognizing that life is finite.

Recognizing the estrangement that characterizes existence and the threat of final separation posed by death, persons draw upon their essential nature—their essence that serves as the standard of judgment of their estrangement—and seek to overcome their alienation from the very ground of being from which they are separated. Yet all attempts to reestablish unity with being itself will fail because all free initiatives are thwarted by the condition of sin, by the structure of estrangement that is part of existing. The persistent pursuit of New Being is a quest for all persons. It is not tied to the historic, covenantal religions of Judaism, Christianity, and Islam, Tillich asserts. For Hindus and Buddhists, among other practitioners, strive to experience unity with the divine "above" history.

What distinguishes Christianity from these other traditions that pursue union with the ground of being from which their practitioners are separated is that Christians affirm the fulfillment of this quest as already having been achieved within history. While other faiths, such as Judaism, experience the promise of fulfillment in history but await its realization, Christians believe that the consummation has already occurred. They identify it with the paradox of New Being as revealed in Jesus as the Christ. In him, the truly universal (the ground and power of being) and the unmistakably concrete (that which exists) coincide. The Christian assertion that New Being has appeared in Jesus as the Christ is neither irrational nor absurd, but paradoxical. This fundamental paradox of "eternal God-manhood" contradicts "the whole of ordinary human experience, including the empirical and the rational."[6] It is also the foundation for all of the other paradoxical elements affirmed in Christianity. Like all symbols that provide a surplus of meaning that cannot be fully explicated in discursive language, the symbol of the Christ exceeds full human comprehension while it discloses human essence.

Because of his desire to emphasize the symbolic character and power of the Christ event, Tillich preferred to use the phrase "Jesus as the Christ" to refer to the historic appearance of Jesus of Nazareth and his manifestation of New Being. The certainty of the revelation is not subject to scientific or historic verification, for the true test of Christian faith lies in the witness of persons who have been transformed by the reception and experience of Jesus as the Christ. While the fullness of New Being is disclosed in the messianic work of Jesus of Nazareth, the experience of New Being cannot be confined to those who know the name of Jesus. New Being is essential being—the intended being of creation—expressing itself and acting within the strictures of existence. Simply, wherever the estranged experience of persons is overcome in love, New Being is present. Nonetheless, Tillich affirms that *as* New Being, Jesus as the Christ fully and finally overcomes the constraints and disruptions of existence—its estrangement from the ground of being itself and its penchant for self-destruction.

Rather than use the traditional Chalcedonian metaphorical language about the divine and human natures combined in the Christ, Tillich prefers more dynamic language that focuses on the eternal God-human unity. In this way Tillich avoids the tendency of theologians to identify the incarnation as a single, temporal event. At the very least, the incarnation for Tillich does not mean that God has become human. Instead, for him the incarnation is a symbol that expresses the eternal event of the fullness of the relationship between being itself and human life—the fullness uniquely manifest in the life and work of Jesus, in whom essential humanity experienced reality in existence without succumbing to its limits. Thus, Jesus becomes the Christ, the *Logos* that was the full and dynamic presence of being itself while participating completely in the human predicament. "Only by taking suffering and death upon himself could Jesus be the Christ," Tillich reasons, "because only in this way could he participate completely in existence and conquer every force of estrangement which tried to dissolve his unity with God."[7]

The stories of Jesus repelling the temptations of food, knowledge, and power, Tillich insists, are symbolic ways in which his followers relate his goodness and sinlessness, the recognition that as New Being, Jesus was not estranged from being itself. Humans are able to participate in New Being because it is—because Jesus as the Christ was—New Being. "Being Christlike," as Tillich puts it, "means participating fully in the New Being present in him."[8] At this point Tillich resonates with the affirmation of Paul in 2 Corinthians 5:17: "So if anyone is in Christ, there is a new creation: everything old has passed away; see, everything has become new!" In this way Tillich affirms that Jesus as the Christ fulfills the messianic role as the criterion against which all existents are judged—measuring the disjunctions between their essence and their actual existence. For this reason, then, Tillich is able to identify that Jesus as the Christ is the center of history.

Tillich understands the incarnation as a symbol; so too he identifies the cross and the resurrection as symbols of the reconciliation effected by Jesus as the Christ. The "Cross of Christ" is the most powerful symbolic expression of the subjection of New Being to the strictures and disruptions of finitude; and the "Resurrection of Christ" is similarly the most powerful symbolic expression of New Being's conquest of the limits of finitude. To a very real extent, since the crucifixion was a historical event, the cross of Christ is an event that became a symbol. And because of the transformative experience of New Being in the lives of early disciples, the resurrection became a symbol for the new life that was possible in Christ. For Tillich, the event of the cross became a central Christian symbol, while the transformation symbolized by resurrection assumed the character of an event.

Tillich clusters most biblical stories and symbols about Jesus around these two symbols of the cross and the resurrection. Among those that he associates with the cross are accounts of Jesus' birth, his family's poverty, and their flight into Egypt.[9] Each of these events underscores the lowly estate of Jesus, his separation from the mainstream of Jewish society, and his early suffering. By embedding Jesus in the difficult conditions of existence—poverty, loneliness, and the violence that drove his family into Egypt—the stories display that New Being was challenged with the extreme threats of existence.

He also identifies other accounts of biblical miracles with an existential appropriation of the resurrection. For starters, Tillich suggests that the texts about the preexistence of the Christ (as in the prologue to the Gospel of John and the kenotic hymn in Phil. 2:5-11) are symbols that anticipate the resurrection. In addition, Tillich associates images and stories of miracles, the ascension, Pentecost, the millennium, the second coming, and final judgment with the core symbol of the resurrection, from which each of these symbols draws significance.[10] For instance, the stories of the miracles are not challenges to the scientific laws of nature; instead, they are narratives that dramatize the power of New Being to overcome the limits of existence, to conquer the self-destructive tendencies in human relationships, and to revive the essential being that is intended for reality. Similarly, the expectation of the second coming affirms that New Being not only has defeated death as the final limit of finitude; it also affirms that, during the period of awaiting the Parousia, Jesus as the Christ cannot be superseded by another being in history.

The reconciling and redeeming work of the Christ is one for which salvation is eternal—not in terms of its temporality, but in terms of its depth. For Tillich, salvation is the process of "essentialization," which means that salvation exposes the negative as negative and celebrates the positive as positive. As such, salvation is the existential experience of New Being. It deepens one's experience of being and, in so doing, restores humans' relationships with God and enriches the prospects for human relationships in loving each other. In salvation—in healing—one is transformed from old being to the new creation in Christ that Paul celebrated in his second epistle to the Corinthians.

The New Being is new in three senses of re-newal: re-conciliation, re-union, and re-surrection.[11] In the process of reconciliation, the relationship with God—with being itself—is restored, and the reconciliation with Being also means that one is reconciled with oneself (experiencing wholeness) and with others (experiencing true community). When reconciliation occurs, Tillich asserts in one of his sermons, "one feels united with God, the ground and meaning of one's existence." This experience of reunion with Being and with oneself generates the courage to confront anxiety and facilitates a deep self-acceptance. Finally, the experience of resurrection is not projected into the future following physical death; instead, "it is the power of the New Being to create life out of death, here and now, today and tomorrow." And, Tillich continues, "resurrection happens now, or it does not happen at all. It happens in us and around us, in soul and history, in nature and universe."[12]

Although participation in New Being is the existential experience of salvation—of healing—it is never complete because of the conditions of existence. Throughout the human experience of reconciliation, reunion, and resurrection, Jesus as the Christ—the model of New Being—is the ultimate criterion against which the healing and saving process is measured. In short, the New Being of the Christ is the work of reconciliation, and the work of reconciliation is the full expression of New Being, of reunion with being itself, of experiencing a new or resurrected life.

Unlike many Christian theologians, Tillich is less concerned about the historical life and acts of Jesus of Nazareth than he is about the meaning of the Christ—the New Being—as it is revealed and perceived in the testimonies of the Gospels and from believers. In particular, in two striking ways he distinguishes his Christology from that of most Christian theologians. First, he locates the "expectation" for the appearance of the Christ not in the prophecies of Hebrew Scriptures but in human essence—in the ideal of "dreaming innocence" that informs existence. Second, he understands the significant messianic events identified with the life and ministry of Jesus of Nazareth as being symbolic. In particular, he focuses on the virgin birth, the miracles, the cross, the resurrection, and the second coming as symbols. The symbolic recognition of these events does not preclude their possible historic grounding, but it does not require an affirmation of their historicity.

Tillich's Christology is a crucial component of his theology because New Being is the power to overcome the estrangement that humans experience as a condition of their existence and the penchant to sin. For wherever love is present, reuniting separated persons from each other and from being itself, there New Being exerts its power of reconciliation, which is the ultimate work of the Christ.

Questions for Reflection

1. Tillich avers that human existence is fraught with alienation, ambiguity, and estrangement. How adequate or inadequate are terms like these to describe the biblical notion of sin?

2. Is Tillich's view of "Jesus as the Christ" an adoptionist Christology?

CHAPTER SIX

LIFE, ITS AMBIGUITIES, AND THE QUEST FOR UNAMBIGUOUS LIFE

How is a community of faith possible without suppression of the autonomy of man's spiritual life?[1]

In part 4 of *Systematic Theology*, "Life and the Spirit," Paul Tillich takes up the questions of life, its ambiguities, and the quest for unambiguous life.[2] First, he delineates the dimensions, functions, and questions of life. Then, he answers the questions of life with a discussion of three theological symbols that are frequently taken literally by many theologians: the symbols of Holy Spirit, the kingdom of God, and eternal life, each of which provides nonliteral theological answers to the questions of life under the canopy of a new term, *Spiritual Presence*.

Tillich understands life in ontological terms, as containing both an essential/potential pole and an existential/actual pole. The former aspect refers to the unambiguous power of being. The latter aspect refers to life under the conditions of existence, beset by finitude, estrangement, conflict, and anxiety. Life is a "mixture" of the ideal and the real, or the potential and the actual.[3]

Tillich speaks of the polar structure of life as a multidimensional unity.[4] Like Teilhard de Chardin, he understands the inorganic and organic dimensions of reality not as separate realms but as interrelated in a continuum from nonliving to living. Dimensions are structured in terms of their place in time, space, causality, and substance.[5] As far as is known, animal life alone operates as self-aware—self-related, self-preserving, self-increasing, and self-continuing "living wholes."[6] Only humans manifest self-awareness and dwell in the dimension of the personal-communal, or the dimension of Spiritual Presence,[7] which is the power of life. It is not a "part" of the human; it is rather the unity of life-power and life in meaning, or the unity of power and meaning.[8] In short, spirit pervades life in all its aspects.

Tillich distinguishes three principal functions of life: *self-integration* with the principle of centeredness, *self-creativity* with the principle of growth, and *self-transcendence* with the principle of sublimity. He then explicates how these three functions participate in the three polarities of the structure of being.

First, the integrative or centering function is a quality of individualization in the self-actualization of life. Because of the ambiguity of existence, the quest for centeredness, or integration, may result in disintegration, meaning the failure to become centered. The spiritual dimension in the activation of centeredness is morality in which the centered self constitutes itself as a person.[9]

Second, the self-creativity—or growing function—is a quality of dynamics and form, involving the polarity of an established center (form) whose aim is to grow or develop (dynamics). Growth may be creative, but it may also be destructive and bring chaos.[10] Tillich states, "The moment of our conception is the moment in which we begin not only to live but also to die."[11] The spiritual dimension in the activation of self-creativity is culture, including growth enhancers such as language, art, and technology, which seek the development of all existents to actualize their potential.[12]

The third polarity is the locus of religion that Tillich defines as life under the dimension of spirit. Living is the self-actualization of one's potential in a finite and, thus, ambiguous world, and the quest for unambiguous life. Although Tillich employs nontraditional language, he refers in this section to the customary concepts of creation, fall, and redemption.

The dimension of spirit is, of course, Tillich's focus. In this dimension one's self-transcendence drives toward the union of the finite self with the essential self. This drive is the heart of religion or, more precisely, being religious. It is life under the dimension of spirit. Because humans are conscious and self-conscious, they are aware of both the ambiguities of life and the quest for unambiguous life. In religion this quest begins. It is the quest for God, Essential Being, which in the covenantal religions is encountered through revelation.

Because God is in all dimensions of life, God is immanently and essentially present everywhere. While humans seek to know and experience their essential ground—the depth of their being—and while they are fully aware of their alienation from their being in finite existence, the "answer" to their quest is the revelation of God in the human ecstasy of self-transcendence. Being "in Christ" (a Pauline staple that refers to one's experience of God) is the state of being grasped by the unity of unambiguous life (which is the heart of faith) and the unity of the broken and alienated self (which is the sense of love). In Christianity, sacraments and the Word are the media through which faith and love emerge.

Tillich refers to Spiritual Presence (the capital letters refer to the traditional concept of God as Spirit) to describe the "God experience." Essentially, God is present in all dimensions of life, as the ground of all. When humans ask about the nature and meaning of life, thus posing the spiritual question, God answers in the ecstasy of the revelation of Spiritual Presence, which is the experience of eternal life. Spiritual Presence reunites the separated and estranged self in its essential unity as the centered self, the symbol of the kingdom of God.

In the concluding portion of *Systematic Theology* 3, Tillich elaborates on spiritual community (the church) and spiritual life (individuals and communities living as participants in the kingdom of God). First, he discusses spiritual community.[13] Noting that Spiritual Presence is manifested through sacraments and Word actually, Tillich regards everything in existence as potentially sacramental, as a possible vehicle of grace. This sacramental potential exists because all objects participate in Being. Both natural and human objects can mediate the essential elements of reality and evoke the ecstasy of reunion in Spiritual Presence. In the New Testament, the Gospel of John is replete with illustrations of the symbolic abilities of nature. In water and wine, for example, objects become windows of grace. Of course, as the spiritual community developed in history, specific rites, like baptism and the Eucharist became the central media for grace.[14] In addition to ritual acts, Spiritual Presence is evoked through speech-acts that attempt to explain the meaning of faith. Sermons or homilies are primary linguistic tools in Christianity to stimulate the experience of grace; thus, the notion of the "power" of the Word through spoken words plays a central role in the spiritual dimension.

Essentially, life in spiritual community, or ecclesial life, is marked by five characteristics: ecstasy, faith, love, unity, and universality. These marks mirror the historic church's classic marks of spiritual life, namely, the claim that the church is one, holy, catholic, and apostolic.

These unambiguous marks are, in real churches, actually ambiguous. The church is not "The Church" in actuality. It is both a theological (unambiguous) and a sociological (ambiguous) entity. Spiritual Presence is the essential heart of actual churches if, and when, they manifest the grace, love, and power of Being. At the same time, the church may, and often does, reflect features that distort churches' core values.

In *The Dynamics of Faith*, for example, Tillich differentiates three tendencies in churches that have resulted in skewed concrete expressions of the life of a church.[15] Each tendency results in a distortion of the unambiguous experience of Spiritual Presence. The *intellectualist distortion* tends to reduce faith to assent to the authority of the church (the Roman Catholic tendency) or the authority of the Bible (the Protestant tendency). In these cases, faith's certitude is reduced to the cognitive submission to the teachings of the church or the Bible. The *emotionalistic distortion* tends to reduce faith to an emotional experience that is devoid of rational content. In this distortion human feeling becomes one's authority. The *volunteristic distortion* tends to reduce faith to an act of the will through which one "decides" what is ultimate based on the claim of an external or internal authority or experience. In all three cases, the alleged objectivity of an inerrant authority, the subjective assurance of psychological assurance, or the authenticity of an external authority is elevated to a false authority.

For Tillich, in faith and the life of spiritual community, a balance between objectivity and subjectivity is required. Living faith must have a Catholic substance and a Protestant principle. That is, neither sacrament nor Word alone can be ritualized or codified as an absolute authority. Rather, while the holy is revealed through sacrament, the sacramental act is not holy in itself. Although the Word reveals truth, the words of the Bible, creeds, and sermons are not holy in themselves.

With these principles of spiritual life in place, Tillich addresses the dilemma of conflicting claims for spiritual truth among the world religions. Early interpreters of Tillich often saw him as an exclusivist because he held on christological grounds that only Christianity can claim validity as the true faith. Indeed, as a Christian, Tillich adamantly avers that the one and only criterion by which one can measure the veracity of ultimate commitment is the criterion of Jesus as the Christ. In a vigorous and seemingly ultra-exclusive statement, Tillich claims:

> The final revelation, the revelation in Jesus as the Christ, is universally valid, because it includes the criterion of every revelation and is the finis or telos (intrinsic aim) of all of them. The final revelation is the criterion of every revelation which precedes or follows. It is the criterion of every religion and of every culture, not only of the culture and religion in and through which it has appeared. It is valid for the social existence of every

human group and for the personal existence of every human individual.... If some element is cut off from the universal validity of the message of Jesus as the Christ, if he is put into the sphere of personal achievement only, or into the sphere of history only, he is less than the final revelation and is neither the Christ nor the New Being. But Christian theology affirms that he is all this because he stands the double test of finality: Uninterrupted unity with the ground of his being and the continuous sacrifice of himself as Jesus to himself as the Christ.[16]

The Christian theologian explores and evaluates all religions and quasi religions from this seemingly exclusivist perspective. Some theologians—Tillich especially notes Karl Barth in this respect—and many Christians throughout history have interpreted the Christian priority in an absolutist way, as not one way but the only way. Additionally, like Barth, they have denounced world religions as false or incomplete revelations.[17]

Unlike Barth, however, Tillich maintains a dialectical focus on world religions and quasi religions, rejecting them when they contradict Christianity, yet considering and embracing some of their forms, claims, and practices.[18] In fact, Tillich argues that the dialectic of rejection and acceptance was the predominant Christian view until the eleventh century, when an absolute exclusivism gained prominence for political and polemical reasons. Tillich surveys the relationship of Israel's religion to pagan gods, the teachings of Jesus, Paul's mutual rejection and acceptance of aspects of paganism and Judaism, and the early *Logos* theology at Alexandria as evidence of the "preparatory character of [other] religions," emphasizing how they asked questions from a nascent intimation of truth.[19] Thus, according to Tillich, rather than being exclusive, early Christianity was more appropriately inclusive, rejecting other ways, but simultaneously modifying and adapting pagan forms and content within the structures of Christian faith. What he calls an "astonishing universalism," based on the *Logos* doctrine that posited the entire universe's grounding in God, gave Christianity the ability to be particular, but not insular; confessional, but open to other ways.

This position is entirely commensurate with Tillich's position that the church is the recipient of absolute revelation and a finite and social institution that is both fallible and ambiguous. Thus, the early church set the tone for what Tillich believes is the normative position of Christianity with respect to the world religions, that of critical inclusivism.

Having dealt with the early church's attitudes toward other religions, Tillich rehearses the ways that Christianity has accepted parts of other traditions, for example, the texts of Judaism, the Stoic ethics in Paul, the worship forms from the Gnostics and mystery religions, and the language and concepts of the Greco-Roman Empire. Christianity has also been open to hear and respond to the polemics of other ways, for instance, the criticism from Judaism that Christianity rejected monotheism and the pagan critique that Christianity had profaned the world.[20]

Moreover, following the Protestant principle, the church has been self-critical. Thus, Christianity has not only been in an encounter with other religions, but it has also encountered itself. Tillich finds copious evidence of this discovery in the Hebrew prophets' attack against Israel's religious and political leaders, in Jesus' appeal to a "higher law" (the law of love), and the Reformation's critique of church authority and ritual.[21] If the religions (and quasi religions) would enter into mutual external criticism and internal critique, Tillich believes they would create "a community of conversation which will change both sides of the dialogue."[22]

Because God is the ground of being, and therefore the ground of everything in finite existence, God can in principle be known by all people. Tillich agrees that all persons who seriously respond to objects, events, or persons whom they perceive as vehicles of the sacred are in communion with the heart of reality, with Being, with God, in principle, and sometimes, in a sense, but not directly with the universal revelation in Jesus as the Christ.

In the preface to his 1963 volume *Christianity and the Encounter of the World Religions*, Tillich wrote that he hoped he would "arouse critical thought not only with respect to the relation of Christianity to the world religions but also with respect to its own nature."[23] Although it cannot be claimed that Tillich alone set the foundation for future encounters of the religions of the world, it is indisputable that he has been a valuable theorist on the topic. Still today, his views are relevant to the current situation of religions. Moreover, his insistence that faith traditions be self-reflective has been a catalyst for self-reform and openness to dialogue between faith traditions. Tillich's understanding of religion in general and his particular commitment to Christianity provided him with a complex conceptual basis to address the question of Christianity's relationship to other religions and quasi religions.

Given Tillich's notion of religion as ultimate concern, he focused considerable attention on threatening quasi religions, movements, and ideologies that were not traditionally considered religions. Tillich gave attention to the "religious" ideologies of nationalism (especially fascism and communism), scientism, and liberal humanism, which were growing in an increasingly secular Western culture where the power and authority of Christianity were waning. Now, in ways he both could and could not imagine, quasi religions have become increasingly important in contemporary culture.

Tillich's approach to Christianity's encounter with other religions (especially Judaism and Buddhism) and quasi religions is rooted in his understanding of the dynamics of religion. As always, he begins with a concept of religion as "the state of being grasped by an ultimate concern."[24] In the religions, the name of this concern is God, or the gods, a sacred object, an all-pervading power, or a highest principle. In the quasi religions the ultimate concern is based in a finite entity that can be located in an ideology community, or secular "faith."

The quasi religions have an unintended similarity to the world religions. In nationalism the ultimate concern is the status and viability of the nation. Fervor and commitment attend this concern. Stories of the nation and its founders take on "sacred" status. Events, places, and leaders become symbols of the profound meaning of the nation. National rites have the form and function of sacred rituals. Founding documents become authoritative words. The national ethos becomes a way of life providing moral compass. One lives in the nation and for the nation and defends the nation.[25]

Questions for Reflection

1. To what extent is Tillich's ecclesiology pertinent to the emergent church?
2. What are the implications of Tillich's view of spiritual acceptance?
3. What is at issue theologically and ecclesially in speaking of Spiritual Presence instead of the Holy Spirit?

CHAPTER SEVEN

HISTORY AND THE KINGDOM OF GOD

The christological question is the question of Christ as the center of history.[1]

For centuries in Western cultures, two models for conceiving history dominated thought. One was a cyclical model derived from the Greco-Roman historians, and the other was a linear model developed from Jewish and Christian understanding of God's role in directing humans through time. In the past two centuries, however, a third viable model has achieved prominence, one that is dialectical or mythical. For the most part, dialectical interpretations were put forth by late nineteenth- and early twentieth-century liberals who thought that humans were progressively improving, moving irreversibly toward the perfection of history.

Reacting strongly against the liberal optimism of a progressive understanding of history, Paul Tillich desired to show two things: first, history does not contain or generate its own meaning, nor does it, of its own accord or human activity, progress toward its *telos*; and second, history is, nevertheless, never without the presence of teleological meaning. To make his argument, Tillich introduces the concept of *kairos*, which refers to "the right time" or "the time of fulfillment of an action." For him, the paradigmatic *kairos* is the appearance of Jesus as the Christ, the introduction of New Being into the historical order. The Christ event is not generated by history, which means that history does not develop or determine its own meaning. For Tillich, the Christ event also manifests the ultimate meaning of history and thereby establishes the criterion by which the relative meaning of all other historical events is judged.

The foundation for Tillich's concept of history is derived from his understanding of the Greek idea *historia*, which means "primarily inquiry, information, report, and only secondarily the events inquired about."[2] From this understanding of *historia*, Tillich draws the basis for his idea of the polar structure of history, identified as subjective and objective foci. In this dialectic, the subjective side is dominant because interpretation, in a sense, precedes the recognition of events as history. Historical consciousness does not temporally precede the event that it interprets, but it does transform mere happenings into historical events. Since historical consciousness identifies and describes historical events, history is necessarily human history, in contrast to notions about natural history in the process of evolution; only humans possess the consciousness required for transforming raw events into *historical* occasions. Yet as Tillich says, "There is no history without factual occurrences, and there is no history without the reception and interpretation of factual occurrences by historical consciousness."[3]

A second indication of the human character of history—and thus its social character—is that interpretation occurs only in the context of tradition, which is a collection of remembered, significant events for a particular group. Epics, sagas, and legends, for instance, have historical roots, and they express remembered events in a symbolic manner. Modern attempts to demythologize history depend upon a tradition of symbol interpretation in which historians participate.

History is human history in yet a third sense. At each moment in a tradition, numerous occurrences offer themselves as potential objects for being recognized and recorded as historical events. The act of determining which events merit historical status depends on the values of a specific historical group and its tradition. Again, the social nature of human existence is intertwined with the basic characteristic of history.

In these three ways the human character of history is determined by its subjective element. But like the subjective element of history, the objective element draws its distinct characteristics from human historical consciousness. In the first place, the decisive factor that a raw event can become historical is human purpose. Although human intention may not be actualized in a raw event, the presence of human purpose is the decisive factor for all events that become history. A second constitutive factor of historical events is the element of human freedom, which interjects itself into an evolving sequence. Third, because human freedom acts upon and within the given conditions of a historical situation, the "new" is produced. The processes of nature also produce the new, such as a new species in the evolutionary process. But a qualitative difference exists between the natural forms of the new and the new produced in history, because the new that results from the interplay between human freedom and given conditions primarily concerns meaning and value. For Tillich, the final characteristic of the objective aspect of history proper is its "significant uniqueness," which grows out of his theological understanding of existence and human life. It also provides a context for his consideration of the kingdom of God and its transformative modeling, both for this world and for teleological hope. In addition, history provides the temporal context for the appearance of New Being, the revelation of divine reality and the restoration of the intended relation between persons and God. Finally, in line with Tillich's method of correlation, history poses questions for which theology then provides answers.

According to Tillich, the components of the structure of history correspond to the categories of being and existence—time, space, causality, and substance, with time manifesting singular importance. For him, there is no overarching category of time that is the same in all dimensions of being and existence. Instead, within each distinct dimension there is a certain category of time. As he puts it, "Time is both an independent and a relational concept: time remains time in the whole realm of finitude; but the time of the amoeba and the time of historical man are different."[4]

Although history is a dimension that moves beyond temporality itself, history is a human creation that embraces an understanding of time as always moving forward—time as inescapably, irreversibly, and unrepeatably moving toward what is new. The beginning and the ending of historical time are determined by the center of historical time—the "locus where the *meaning* of the temporal process has been actualized objectively for a moment and in such a way that it not only gives meaning to the whole but also determines backward, the beginning; and forward, the end."[5] By contrast, an existential sequence or "natural time," which is the reality of events occurring in a sequential fashion, has neither a beginning nor an end. When this existential sequentiality is attributed the characteristics of beginning and ending, it is confused with historical time, which deals with the symbols of creation and of the eschaton.

Within the dimension of history, "time tears itself away from space" and establishes predominance over it.[6] The categories of causality and substance have a special relation to the historical dimension of being. Historical causality encompasses all other forms of causality because all other dimensions of life actively participate in the historical realm, which is always future oriented, always creating the new. Like the category of historical causality, historical substance—or the historical situation—bears a unique relation to the historical dimension of life. Historical substance is the "historical situation" in all its multiple and varied manifestations, ranging from the inorganic and organic to the cultural and psychological. The interconnection between historical causality and historical substance reflects the relation between historical time and historical space: the future orientation of historical causality lures historical substance in the direction of the future.

The press of history toward the new engages change, which raises questions about the causes and processes of that movement, about the necessities of reality and the contingencies of possibility. For Tillich, the origin of the element of necessity lies in the historical situation, and the origin of the element of contingency lies in historical causality or its creativity. Contingency and necessity always occur in tandem and in tension, with one usually dominating the other to such an extent that Tillich refers to the occasions dominated by historical necessity as being a "trend" rather than a law. Similarly, he designates the occasions dominated by contingency as "chance." Trends point to the regularities and apparent repetitions within history, which, unlike natural laws, cannot be predicted with scientific certainty. In contrast, chances are occasions that disrupt the determining powers of trends. "Of course," Tillich adds,

> neither chances nor trends are absolute. The determining power of the given situation limits the margin of chances and often makes it very small. Nevertheless, the existence of chances, balancing the determining power of trends, is the decisive argument against all forms of historical determinism—naturalistic, dialectical, or predestinarian.[7]

The movement of history, however, is not limited to the interplay between historical conditions and contingencies.

For Tillich, the ambiguities of historical existence are the means through which history itself seeks fulfillment: self-integration, self-creativity, and self-transcendence. Each of these ambiguities is a form of the basic problem of historical existence, a problem that results from the fact that "history, while running ahead toward its ultimate aim, continuously actualizes limited aims, and in so doing it both achieves and defeats its ultimate aim."[8] The basic ambiguity of history, then, is the substitution and realization of penultimate goals in place of the ultimate aim of history. Consequently, the answer to the problem of history must come from beyond history itself.

First, in history, the ambiguity of self-integration is evident in the formation of empires, which exhibit two fundamental characteristics—the will to power and a vocational self-interpretation. The will to power develops the cohesiveness required of all history-bearing groups. And the vocational self-interpretation of an empire gives it a focused aim. As examples of the vocational self-interpretation of empires, Tillich cites America's self-understanding as the representative of liberty, ancient Rome's as the representative of the law, and Victorian England's as the representative of Christian civilization. In and of themselves, the vocational self-interpretations of empires are neither good nor evil, although historical evidence reveals that extensive suffering and destruction of the structures of meaning have been caused in the name of an empire's vocational self-interpretation.

Second, the historical ambiguity of self-creativity appears most frequently in the realm of political activity. The basis of this ambiguity lies in the process of creativity, wherein the new emerges from the old. Regardless of the radicality or similarity of the new to the old form, its roots lie within the old.

The third historical ambiguity is that of self-transcendence. It represents the most destructive stage of the ambiguity of self-creativity, which occurs when either the old or the new lays claim to ultimate worth. Not only do political factions claim ultimacy; religious groups also are notorious for asserting claims to the final truth. The history of religions reveals that the holy is the favorite sphere for demonic activity, for religious totalitarianism often has wreaked vast destruction and suffering through religiously sanctioned persecution, wars, and genocides.

A group's claim that it possesses ultimacy often is expressed in terms of the anticipated consummation of history, at least of having entered the final stage of history. Belief that the final stage of history has been entered or that it is imminent is not, however, restricted to religious communities. That kind of thinking also finds secular expression in the ideas of the Age of Reason or a classless society, and in the formation of utopian communities. Wherever such a secular or religious attitude is manifest, there looms the danger of the loss of the self-transcendent function of life, either by identifying a symbol of the end of history with the ultimate or by sinking into cynicism and despair about unconsummated utopian expectations.

"The ambiguities of life under the dimension of history and the implication of these ambiguities for the life of the individual within his historical group," Tillich concludes, "lead to the question: What is the significance of history for the meaning of existence universally?"[9] This question, Tillich believes, is the one that all interpretations of history try to answer. It is precisely this question that calls theology to respond with truth.

Consistently, Tillich stresses the ontological character of the interpretation of history by pointing out that "history is the all-embracing dimension of life" and that "the answer to the meaning of history implies an answer to the universal meaning of being."[10] The question about history and its resolution also anticipates the christological question that addresses "the concrete point at which something absolute appears in history and provides it with meaning and purpose."[11] In preparation for proposing his theological answers to the problems of history, Tillich enumerates various inadequate interpretations of history, both negative and positive. Throughout history, he asserts, there have been various negative interpretations of history, ranging from the *tragic* interpretation of the Greeks, who thought of history as ever cycling through conflicts and events, to the *mystical* interpretations propounded by Eastern religions, which suggest that a person needs to transform perceptions of reality, and finally to *reductionistic* interpretations, which attempt to confine history to a chronology of events.

These negative interpretations of history have several common characteristics. Most important, negative interpretations of history use nature as the basis for understanding reality, and as a corollary, they privilege space and substance over time. Thereby they deny that history has an original and independent character, and they regard history as being in the temporal realm of deterioration and decay. These negative interpretations, Tillich concludes, fail to recognize a sense of purpose in historical movement and refuse to see an aim in history.[12]

Tillich also distinguishes three positive forms of historical interpretation, each of which, however, finally proves inadequate in its conclusions. The first is *progressivism*, which suggests unlimited progress without a definite end. Such a hopeful interpretation was demolished by World War I. Similar to progressivism, *utopianism* focuses on the progress of humankind in history, often conceiving the establishment of the utopian community itself as the final movement to usher in the consummation of history. Utopianism, however, fails to account for the human experience of alienation, the ambiguities of history, and the circumstances of its present historical situation.

A third positive form of historical interpretation is often associated with traditional Christian perspectives that feature heavenly reward for individuals after death. This *transcendental* interpretation proves insufficient because it separates the salvation of the individual from the groups in which the individual participates, because it contrasts salvation with creation (effectively eliminating power from redemption), and because it restricts the kingdom of God to a projected experience after life (limiting it to deceased Christians and thus excluding the historical realms of culture and nature from participation in the fulfillment of history).

An adequate theological response to the questions posed by history—its ambiguities of self-integration, self-creativity, and self-transcendence—is provided by the symbol of the kingdom of God. Because of its symbolic character, the kingdom of God has a dual nature as both historical and transhistorical. As historical, the kingdom of God is involved in the dynamics of history, while, as transhistorical, it resolves the ambiguities of the very dynamics of history in which it participates. Furthermore, as a symbol, the kingdom of God embraces and models fulfillment for all spheres of human life—political, social, and personal. Of these, the foremost is the political sphere, which also dominates the dynamics of history. From the political sphere, the symbol the kingdom of God derives its emphasis from the idea that God rules over history. Within the social sphere, the symbol the kingdom of God generates its characteristics of justice and peace, thus fulfilling the utopian expectations for justice and peace and simultaneously liberating them from the relativity of utopianism by acknowledging that they are from God. The symbol the kingdom of God also represents the eternal aim of fulfilling the humanity of every person. And finally, the symbol the kingdom of God is characterized by its universality. Tillich writes, "It is a kingdom not only of men; it involves the fulfillment of life under all dimensions."[13]

To be an adequate answer to the questions of the meaning of history, the symbol the kingdom of God must be simultaneously immanent and transcendent. It expresses its immanence in the symbol Spiritual Presence and its transcendence in the symbol eternal life. On the whole, biblical presentations of the symbol the kingdom of God offer meaningful interpretations of both its immanent and transcendent qualities. In Hebrew Scriptures, for example, many prophets envisioned the kingdom of God as identical with the chosen people or kingdom of Israel. They did emphasize, however, that God was the one who would lead Israel to victory and that God's holy mountain would be the place for people of all realms to worship. But as military defeats and political upheavals within Israel and Judah rocked this naïve confidence in the immanence or historical realization of the kingdom of God, many of the hopes that had been attached to the immanent kingdom were transferred to transhistorical expectations, which were recorded in the apocalyptic writings of the postexilic period. The apocalyptic perspective, in turn, became significant for New Testament expressions of the kingdom of God. In the apocalyptic pictures, the divine mediator of the kingdom of God is no longer portrayed as the historical Messiah, but as the Son of Man. However, the final stages of history are described in terms of the historical situation of the times. The New Testament writings, though, add a new element to the mythical and apocalyptic images of a transcendent or transhistorical concept of the kingdom of God. According to Tillich, the new element is defined by "the inner-historical appearances of Jesus as the Christ and the foundation of the church in the midst of the ambiguities of history."[14]

Because the symbol the kingdom of God provides meaningful resolution to the ambiguities of history, Tillich concludes that it maps out the course of salvation for history. Yet the history of the revelation of the kingdom of God within history is not an intrinsic part of history; instead, it "breaks into history, works through history, but is not created by history."[15] Where the kingdom of God is manifest in history, both revelation and salvation are present. And the definitive revelation of the kingdom of God, Tillich asserts, occurred with the revelation of Jesus as the Christ at the "center of history," not in the sense of being its chronological midpoint, but the focus of its meaning. This recognition of the center of history means that

> the center of consciousness always lies in the past. It cannot be sought in
> the future, for the meaning of the future is determined by it.... But the cen-
> ter cannot lie in the present either. The present has historical meaning only
> if it is the point in which are joined the historical fate which is born in the
> past and the historical decision which provides the future.[16]

The center of history also determines the beginning and end of history. The beginning of history is the event in which the first stage starts to develop toward the center of history, and the end of history is the goal of the process for which the center is the defining event. Therefore, Tillich concludes, the range of history is determined by the potency of its center.

Within Christian theology, the concept of Christology is specifically attached to the appearance of Jesus as the Christ, a historical event "for which everything before and after is both preparation and reception." As the center of history, the appearance of Jesus as the Christ becomes "both criterion and source of the saving power in history."[17] Recognizing the historical centrality of the event of Jesus as the Christ, Tillich conceives the historical manifestations, partial though they might be, of the kingdom of God as forming a coherent, meaningful series of events. By focusing on its center as the source of history's meaning, Tillich disparages progressive theories of revelation because all events that follow the center both stand in its judgment and draw their meaning from the center, not the *telos* toward which history might be aiming. Although Tillich does not believe in a progressive revelation, he does accept the possibility of progress in the reception of the revelation that appeared at the center of history.

Throughout the past two millennia, manifestations of the kingdom of God have referenced the center of history as the kingdom that was inaugurated in the revelation of Jesus as the Christ. The times when the kingdom has become manifest are experiences of depth, turning points, qualitative experiences rather than quantifiable measures of chronological time. To distinguish these experiences of depth, Tillich uses the Greek concept of *kairos*, which suggests a fulfillment of time. Unlike *chronos*, which denotes a quantifiable measure of time, a *kairos* is a matter of "God's timing," an "involved experience" whose awareness is understood as "a matter of vision."[18] A *kairos* is "the right moment, not any moment, but the particular moment of God's choosing, when time and history are fulfilled."[19] In short, *kairos* is the time of revelation.

Tillich not only applies his concept of *kairos* to the appearance of Jesus as the Christ, which he calls the great, unique, or universal *kairos*, but he also uses the concept in reference to relative *kairoi*, which occur at rare times throughout history when the great *kairos* is reexperienced as the center of history. "*Kairoi* are rare and the great *kairos* is unique, but together they determine the dynamics of history in its self-transcendence."[20] In each of the relative *kairoi*, he declares,

> the "Kingdom of God is at hand," for it is a world-historical, unrepeatable, unique decision for and against the unconditional. Every kairos is, therefore, implicitly the universal kairos and an actualization of the unique kairos, the appearance of the Christ. But no kairos [other than the incarnation of Jesus as the Christ] brings the fulfillment in time.[21]

It follows, then, that the great *kairos*—the Christ, the fullness of revelation, or New Being—functions as both the source of power and the criterion for judgment of all relative *kairoi*. There are, however, two hazards or threats related to *kairoi*: they can be erroneously perceived, and they can be demonically distorted.

In his theology of culture, Tillich identifies the concept of *kairos* with "the coming of a new theology on the soil of a secularized and emptied autonomous culture."[22] For him, a theonomous culture is one that is in every way open to and directed toward the divine. Similarly, a *kairos* is recognized by its openness to the very ground of being that generates and empowers all cultural functions and forms. Simply, *kairoi* reveal New Being and anticipate the kingdom of God in its fullness.

The driving nature of autonomy is always present and active within a theonomous culture. The difference between a theonomous culture and an autonomous one is that, within the autonomous culture, cultural forms and their accretions are seen only in their finite relationships, while those in the theonomous culture are seen in their relationship to the divine. An autonomous culture is concerned with factual, verifiable knowledge, but a theonomous culture is concerned with existential meaning and the ultimate significance of the factual knowledge sought by an autonomous culture. In this way autonomy provides the dynamic of history while theonomy supplies its substance.

The relation between autonomy and theonomy can be seen in the movement of history, which occurs with irregular rhythms, at times seeping slowly and at others rushing rapidly. But the unifying force of history's movement comes from its orientation to theonomous periods that locate its mooring and shape its destiny. The irregular rhythm of history also means that the frequency of *kairoi* cannot be predicted, even though they might be anticipated when things begin to break down in the secular order. Yet even that anticipation of a needed experience of *kairos* during a period of cultural upheaval or disintegration does not guarantee the imminence of its realization.[23] Although the movement of history is irregular and unpredictable, Tillich asserts that the kingdom of God is present in all periods of history, even though its history-shaking power is not always perceived.

One significant component of the symbol the kingdom of God is the idea that God as king is the active ruler of history. Traditionally, the concept of providence has addressed the idea of divine activity in and upon history. Often, however, the concept of providence has merely proved to be a doctrinal disguise for advancing a theory of theological determinism. Tillich refutes two common notions associated with providence: that God manipulates historical events and trends according to a preconceived plan; and that God foresees future events as a spectator, refusing to take an active part in inhibiting works of evil or advancing works of good. Tillich redefines *providence* on the basis of ontological creativity. This perspective affirms God's activity in history by directing it toward its final goal, enhances the roles of human freedom and contingency in history, and includes a realistic understanding of the powers of evil in history.

Tillich conceptually divides the category of ontological creativity into three parts: God's originating creativity, which traditional theologies have treated under the doctrine of creation; God's sustaining creativity, which traditional theologies have treated under the doctrine of preservation; and God's directing creativity, which traditional theologies have treated under the doctrine of providence. By associating providence with divine creativity, Tillich removes the idea of providential activity from familiar assumptions about supernatural interruption and places it within the created order itself. Thus conceived, providence is the inner aim present in all situations; it is the depth of autonomy that presses toward theonomy. The aim of each situation is not conformity with some preconceived design but is, instead, the creation of the genuinely new. In this way of thinking, freedom plays an integral role in the nature of providential activity. The concept of providence does not mean that "divine activity will alter the conditions of finitude and estrangement," but that, drawing upon Paul's testimony in Romans 8, no situation whatsoever can frustrate the fulfillment of a person's ultimate destiny—that nothing can completely separate the person from the love of God in Christ.[24]

For Tillich, providence not only refers to the individual and his or her inner aim (traditionally, "special providence"); it also refers to history as a whole and its inner directedness (traditionally, "historical providence"). Yet special providence and historical providence are not independent categories, for "history in each of its moments, in eras of progress and eras of catastrophe, contributed to the fulfillment of creaturely existence, although this fulfillment does not lie in an eventual time-and-space future."[25]

Additionally, Tillich identifies two deficiencies of idealistic concepts of historical providence. Their primary mistakes are that they use a utopian lens to look for the fulfillment of history within history, and they fail to include aspects of moral and physical evil in their frameworks. Particularly, he eviscerates the progressivistic notions that a future state of historical (or posthistorical) being will repudiate the suffering and injustice encountered throughout history and the naïve assumption that the progression of humankind in such areas as education and technology increases persons' power for good without simultaneously increasing their power for evil.

To countermand such inadequate concepts of historical providence, Tillich thinks of providence not in terms of the fulfillment of history *within* history, but in terms of history's directedness toward fulfillment in the kingdom of God, which features the reconciliation of all existents with the ground and meaning of being. Furthermore, taking evil realistically into account, he reasons that historical providence, because of its nature as inner aim, includes the present and past manifestations of evil. Nevertheless, it creatively presses toward the genuinely new both in history and beyond history. Essentially, then, as Tillich declares in one of his sermons, "Providence means that there is a creative and saving *possibility* implied in every situation, which cannot be destroyed by any event."[26]

Within history, the churches represent the kingdom of God in paradoxical ways: the churches reveal the kingdom of God, but they also conceal its fullness. They must actively support the movement of history toward its aim, and simultaneously they must inhibit and frustrate the profane and demonic attempts to thwart history's intended movement. In order to accomplish this twofold task, the churches derive their power from their consciousness of and participation in the end of history toward which history itself moves, an end that is the fulfillment of the kingdom of God.

The churches also have their own history that pertains to the kingdom of God. Tillich delineates the relation between church history and the kingdom of God as one in which "church history is at no point identical with the kingdom of God and at no point without manifestation of the kingdom of God."[27] Like the general history of the world, church history is not without ambiguities of particularity, wholeness, and integrity. For instance, Tillich suggests the ambiguities by posing the following questions: Why is the church, which is ideally universal, virtually restricted to Western civilization? (At the time that he posed the question, the dramatic growth of Christianity in Asia was in its earliest stages and had not thoroughly developed distinctiveness apart from Western missionary influences.) How could the church give rise to the strongest secular movements in modern history—humanism and communism, which since their emergence have become the greatest rivals to the church? How could the church, which is manifest in many churches, produce numerous conflicting interpretations of the appearance of the Christ? The answers to these paradoxical problems and to the question about the meaning of church history itself lie in the unique nature of church history.

> Since [the church] relates itself in all its periods and appearances to the central manifestation of the Kingdom of God in history, it has in itself the ultimate criterion against itself—the New Being in Jesus as the Christ. The presence of this criterion elevates the churches above any other religious group, not because they are "better" than the others, but because they have a better criterion against themselves and, implicitly, also against other groups.[28]

Church history and its judicial decisions, however, are not isolated from the mainstream of general world history. But the relation between church history and world history is more complex than one merely being a part of the other; for church history is a part of world history and also a part of that which transcends world history—the kingdom of God. The complexity of this relation between church history and world history is intensified by the fact that, using the ultimate criterion of New Being in Jesus as the Christ, church history judges not only itself and other religious communities and their traditions but also world history. And this relation poses yet another paradox: "The churches as representatives of the kingdom of God judge that without which they themselves could not exist."[29] Furthermore, world history is opposed to church history while it also depends upon it for supplying its coherent meaning.

The churches as representatives of the kingdom of God judge history by anticipating and enacting the aim of history. "The fulfillment of history lies in the permanently present end of history, which is the transcendent side of the kingdom of God: the Eternal Life."[30] Even as Tillich clarifies the theological issues related to time in terms of their qualitative dimension rather than quantitative means, so too he shifts the focus of theological concern from the end of history as the cessation of human existence to a consideration of its goal, the depth of its inner aim. By doing so, Tillich relocates the temporal dimensions of eschatology from the future to the present; eschatology becomes an existential concern, for the aim of history underlies, motivates, and exists in every historical moment. To be sure, the future remains an aspect of Tillich's eschatological thinking, but the mode and meaning of the future in eschatological symbolism are identified with the relation of the temporal to the eternal.

Answering the question "What is the relation of history to Eternal Life?" Tillich declares that the "ever present end of history elevates the positive content of history into eternity at the same time that it excludes the negative from participation in it."[31] As a result, that which has been created in history—that which exists—cannot be lost because it has participated in being and thus endures. In eternal life the positive content (that which is identified with being) and the negative (the nonbeing that threatens being) are stripped of their ambiguities, revealing them as they truly are—being and naked nothingness. Eternal life includes the positive content of history but excludes the negative, recognizing it for what it really "is," nonbeing. Eternal life is not a future state of being; instead, Tillich declares, "it is always present, not in man (who is aware of it), but also in everything that has being within the whole state of being."[32] For Tillich, then, eternal life, as the transcendent, symbolic component of the symbol the kingdom of God, is not restricted to humans alone but extends to and includes all portions of the cosmos that have being.

The negative aspect of ultimate judgment—or its condemnation—is seen in the exposure and exclusion of nonbeing from participation in eternal life. But the obverse of ultimate judgment is the transition of the temporal to the eternal, for "the positive in the universe is the object of eternal memory."[33] The positive, however, is not merely the essential nature of a being, for such an understanding (common to both Plato and Schelling) fails to acknowledge the creation of the genuinely new that occurs in history. Yet Tillich uses the concept of essentialization to signify the focus on the positive dimensions of the inner aim of history. The term *essentialization* signifies

> that the new which has been actualized in time and space adds something
> to essential being, uniting it with the positive which is created within exis-
> tence, thus producing the ultimately new, the "New Being," not fragmen-
> tarily as in temporal life, but wholly as a contribution of the kingdom of
> God in its fulfillment.[34]

Essentialization, then, is the process of moving to a new, enriched essence—New Being. It is not limited to persons alone but includes all beings in the universe. As a result, participation in eternal life by any being depends "on a creative synthesis of a being's essential nature with what it has made of its temporal existence."[35] Therein lies the moral dimension of judgment for persons based on their use of their existence.

Tillich concludes that often there have been two characteristics associated with eternal life, even when it has been conceived as "after life." These two characteristics are unification and purification. Unification with God is the restoration of the in-tended relationship of God with humans; and purification does not mean the cleans-ing of personal taints and errors, but the overcoming of distortions of meaning.[36] Thus, the kingdom of God in its transcendent dimension of eternal life serves as the ground of meaning for all historical activity and at the same time judges historical activity, separating positive acts from negative distortions by embracing the positive while exposing the negative in its true nature—nonbeing. In this act of ultimate judg-ment, the kingdom of God completely conquers the ambiguities of life and exerts dominion over the whole of history.

Questions for Reflection

1. If history is human history, in what sense can one consider God as the God of his-tory or as God working in history?
2. What are the ambiguities of history if they are not suspicions about the factual char-acter of events?
3. How is the kingdom of God an adequate answer to the question about the meaning of history?
4. Why are *kairoi* significant to theology, and why are they so rare?
5. What is the relation between history and eternal life?

CHAPTER EIGHT

FAITH AND TRUTH

Faith is the state of being ultimately concerned.[1]

If faith is understood as being ultimately concerned, doubt is a necessary element in it. It is a consequence of the risk of faith.[2]

The truth which does not disappoint dwells below the surfaces in the depth.[3]

In popular religious usage, the term *faith* suggests the pattern of believing in an assertion that somehow ignores reason or requires acceptance without empirical or logical evidence. In short, faith is often associated with one's belief in some phenomenal assertion accepted as true because of the confidence in the person or source making the declaration, or because it resonates, however incredible it might seem, with one's personal experience. For Paul Tillich, however, the concept of faith refers to something much more comprehensive than a doctrinal affirmation. It identifies a way of life, a centered locus for oneself in the world of competing challenges and values. Simply, faith is a matter of being grasped by an ultimate concern and, in response, focusing completely on one's ultimate concern. The "state of being ultimately concerned," Tillich asserts, is true faith. For "whatever concerns a man ultimately becomes god for him, and, conversely, it means that a man can be concerned ultimately only about that which is god for him."[4] Thus, the condition of orienting one's life toward that which concerns one ultimately is the heart of faith.

Faith does not require that one affirm revealed truths, contravene scientific conclusions, or deny reason. "There is no conflict," Tillich declares, "between faith in its true nature and reason in its true nature."[5] Faith requires more than mere assent to propositions, assertions, and revelations. It also cannot be reduced to a person's allegiances and preferences that might reflect embedded cultural values, educational indoctrination, economic privilege, or emotional security. Faith, Tillich avers, is not subject to casual or causal changes in attitude or affection. Instead, faith involves the whole person. It is experienced in the convergence of the volitional, intellectual, emotional, and physical aspects of the entire person. Tillich especially associates faith with the Deuteronomic command that "you shall love the LORD your God with all your heart, and with all your soul, and with all your might" (Deut. 6:5). In the condition of faith as being ultimately concerned, one is grasped and possessed by the ultimate concern.

The pursuit of truth focuses the need for examining the relation between faith and truth. For one thing, Tillich's recognition of the creative role of doubt within faith, rather than opposed to faith, prompts him to consider how the truth of faith can embrace doubt. For another, Tillich wants to distinguish the truth of faith from its misperceived and mislabeled "conflict" with science.

In his discussion of truth in *The Dynamics of Faith*, Tillich treats scientific, historical, and philosophical forms of truth in their relation to faith because, in part, the claims of science, the facts of history, and the propositions of philosophy are often portrayed as challenges to or conflicts with faith. This trinity of truths—scientific, historical, and philosophical—is not an exhaustive list of the forms of truth that Tillich recognizes. Elsewhere he alludes to and reflects upon artistic and mythic forms of truth. Each of these forms of truth, he determines, is distinct in terms of its origin and realm of reference.

In general, Tillich deals with the traditional challenge of reason to the truth claims of Christian theology, particularly as scholars locate the sources of particular truths in science, history, and philosophy. Even so, he is wary about the often restrictive manner and scope of their scholarly pursuits, which often demean religion as mere emotion and belittle poetry as simply aesthetic while privileging science as a kind of natural—and hence most, or only, authentic—truth. When these scholars are asked whether the truth for which they quest is relevant to their lives, they often express a sense of loss or indifference to their newly perceived truths.

The truths of faith and the truths of science, Tillich boldly asserts, do not belong to the same realm of meaning. Their referents and their forums for discussion are distinct: "Science has no right and no power to interfere with faith, and faith has no power to interfere with science."[6] The truth of a scientific statement or law is known by the adequacy of its description of the laws of nature or the structural principles of reality, and the truth of a scientific discovery can be verified by experimental repetition. Always subject to the scientific process of experimentation, the truths of science are consequently and consistently subject to revision, as evinced in the Copernican revolution and the paradigm shift from Newton's laws to Einstein's theories of relativity. As a result, the truths of science can conflict only with scientific principles, since "science which remains science cannot conflict with faith which remains faith."[7] The political conflicts between evolutionary theorists and proponents of "intelligent design" are not struggles between science and faith. Instead, they manifest a conflict between science's misappropriation of the human spirit and incorrect projections about the character of revelation and truth.

Even as the truths of science belong to a different realm of reference than those of faith, so too historical truths—or "factual" truths, as Tillich deems them—operate in a frame that is not subject to certification by faith. "But faith," Tillich concludes, "can and must interpret the meaning of facts from the point of a view of a man's ultimate concern. In doing so [faith] transfers historical truth into the dimension of the truth of faith."[8] Although it is possible for the facts of history to be assumed within the realm of faith, it is not possible for the truths of history to contest the truths of faith. Nevertheless, a problem that emerges for Christians involves the degree to which they desire that faith be built upon the certitude of historical facts. Tillich holds that "the truth of faith cannot be made dependent on the historical truth of the stories and legends in which faith has expressed itself. It is a disastrous distortion of the meaning of faith to identify it with the belief in the historical validity of the Biblical stories."[9]

Tillich recognizes that the truth of faith has become entangled with expectations for the affirmations being historically true. It is not a project of faith, for example, for Jews and Christians to determine whether Mosaic passages of the Pentateuch are "sacred legend" rather than "actual history." Nor is it a function of faith for Christians to decide how much of the Gospel narratives about the teachings of Jesus represent early Christian amalgamations of hopes about Jesus and fears about impending political persecution and retribution. Instead, Tillich argues, these questions must be addressed in terms of probability and in terms of historical research because they are questions about human history, about the human writing and transmission of texts.

In contrast to the issues raised in these questions about historical truths, "faith can say that something of ultimate concern has happened in history because the question of the ultimate in being and meaning is involved." And Tillich continues, "Faith includes certitude about its own foundation—for example, an event in history which has transformed history—for the faithful. But faith does not include historical knowledge about the way in which this event took place."[10] In other words, faith deals with the ways that the understanding of events has transformed believers, but it does not make claims about the historical accuracy or verifiability of the event itself. Consequently, the truth of faith cannot be jolted by criticism of historical events and traditions. This acceptance of "the independence of historical truth" is one of the most liberating insights that one can develop from understanding faith as ultimate concern rather than as the affirmation of traditional creeds or stories as dogma.

In addition to his distinction of the truth of faith from scientific and historical truths, Tillich considers how the truth of faith contrasts with philosophical truths. Often this contrast is misunderstood as a conflict between revelation and reason. But a conflict cannot arise when one understands faith in relation to ultimate concern because reason provides intellectual tools for interpreting reality while faith orients the application of those effective, intellectual tools for the analysis and interpretation of reality. "Reason is," Tillich asserts, "the precondition of faith." Reason provides tools for use in direct understanding. The relation of faith to reason is not one of blindness but one of reaching the boundary. When reason, consciously bound by its own limits, reaches beyond that over which it exercises control, it is not completely bound by finitude and rises above it, engaging the infinite, the absolute, being itself. When reason is thus "grasped by an ultimate concern" and "driven beyond itself," it does not void its relational character. Instead, reason becomes ecstatically fulfilled as it is driven beyond its finite limits and experiences the fullness of union with being itself.[11]

For Tillich, the perceived disjunction between faith and reason grows out of a misunderstanding of ways of knowing that is derived from the estrangement that humans experience as a consequence of their existence. A challenge for theology thus becomes one of seeking reconciliation between faith and reason. In this pursuit, theology must question "whether the unity of faith and reason and the true nature of both of them must not be re-established by what religion calls 'revelation.'" And theologians must consistently ask whether "reason in its distorted stage [is] not obliged to subject itself to revelation and . . . [whether] this subjection to the contents of revelation [is] the true sense of the term 'faith.'"[12]

The concept of revelation has also been popularly misunderstood as "divine information about divine matters, given to prophets and apostles and dictated by the divine Spirit to the writers of the Bible, or the Koran, or other sacred books." This errant understanding of revelation then generates the misunderstanding of faith as the "acceptance of such divine informations, however absurd and irrational they may be."

Rightly comprehended, Tillich asserts,

> Revelation is first of all the experience in which an ultimate concern grasps the human mind and creates a community in which this concern expresses itself in symbols of action, imagination, and thought.... Their internal and mutual conflicts are conquered, and estrangement is replaced by reconciliation. This is what revelation means, or should mean. It is an event in which the ultimate becomes manifest in an ultimate concern.... In such an experience no conflict between faith and reason is possible; for it is man's total structure as a rational being which is grasped and changed by the revelatory manifestation of an ultimate concern.[13]

For Tillich, revelation is the occasion of disclosure and discovery when one finds that one's ultimate concern is judged as inadequate or idolatrous because it regards the symbols of faith—of God—as the object or goal of one's faith. Revelation does not impart an ultimate concern where none previously existed. Instead, it purifies, refines, or redirects one's allegiance by focusing on that which is truly ultimate: God.

Although revelation generates an experience of ecstasy in its perception, and although it conquers the corrupted human experience of faith and reason, revelation does not dissolve or otherwise completely remove the disruption. But it does break the final hold of its grip. The corruption of faith and reason persists because finitude itself is the condition of human existence; and finitude is the condition of and for disruption and estrangement—for sin. The corruption of faith and reason "makes faith idolatrous, confusing the bearer and the manifestations of the ultimate with the ultimate itself. It deprives reason of its ecstatic power, of its tendency to transcend itself in the direction of the ultimate."[14] In the distorted relation between faith and reason, persons often consider reason as ultimate despite its finitude, and consequently they demean faith as being preliminary or, to some degree, uninformed.

While Tillich provides a fresh analysis of the relation between faith and reason, so too does he offer a new examination of the relation between faith and doubt. Although traditional theological schemes often characterize doubt as a serious impediment to faith, likely involving its distortion or denial, Tillich considers doubt to be an integral aspect of the condition of faith. "If faith is understood as belief that something is true, doubt is incompatible with the act of faith," he avers. However, "if faith is understood as being ultimately concerned, doubt is a necessary element in it. It is a consequence of the risk of faith."[15] The risk of faith is endemic to the character of faith as ultimate concern, since that which is ultimate can be disclosed and known only through symbols, which, in turn, cannot exactly specify their referent—thus leaving open the creative space for doubt. Even ecstatic experiences of the holy contain the possibility that their origin or goal resides in self-delusion or self-gratification rather than in reconciliation with the ground of being.

In every act of faith there is the possibility of failure, corruption, or deception. Consequently, Tillich insists that certainty evinces idolatry, while doubt indicates faith. As fervently as faith might be expressed, the element of uncertainty cannot be removed or overcome. "Faith is certain in so far as it is an experience of the holy,"

Tillich acknowledges. "But faith is uncertain in so far as the infinite to which it is related is received by a finite being."[16] Growing out of the conditions of finitude, this experience of uncertainty generates the human experience of anxiety. It is finally through courage, Tillich concludes, that faith effectively addresses anxiety and exhibits its dynamic character, incorporating and transforming the destructive potential of doubt into service as the creative prompt for faith itself.[17]

When persons proclaim their certainty as markers of the seriousness or significance of their faith, their arrogance actually suggests the absence of a necessary first step in their thinking about their spiritual life. "The first condition of theological existence," Tillich determines, "is the realization that one does *not* know whether he has experienced the Divine Spirit, or spirits which are not divine."[18] A person's insistence on being absolutely full in faith and completely doubt free is self-deceiving because all persons, whether openly admitting their concerns or not, experience the "permanent threat" of despair in knowing truth. However, a person's acknowledgement of doubt— one's awareness "of the element of insecurity in every existential truth"—manifests an inquisitive orientation that identifies the seriousness of one's faith because, as Tillich reasons, in the depth of every serious doubt and every despair of truth, the passion for truth is still at work. Consequently, Tillich concludes that serious doubt confirms serious faith.[19] In provocative as well as threatening ways, doubt is always necessarily present in experiences of faith, in all human pursuits of liberating truth, and in all experiences of being grasped by the power of being itself.

Related to the issues of doubt and truth, Tillich identifies two "temptations" that confront all who ask questions about whether truth matters. One of these is the threat of indifference, of not caring about matters of truth. This challenge is the way that the majority of modern and contemporary thinkers follow. In times of crisis, in the liminal situations of life involving tragic events (such as the loss of a job, a serious injury or illness, or the failure of a final exam), one finds that the tragic events often spur questions related to ultimate concern. Most persons, however, simply trudge through daily existence by distancing themselves from such serious questions, especially as they apply to oneself.

Distinct from indifference, the other "temptation" is to avoid asking challenging questions about whether truth matters by denying the possibility of articulating the concerns of existential doubt. Addressing dutiful and pious Christians, Tillich challenges them to examine their perceptions and pursuit of truth. He warns that they are not exempt from the structure of doubt merely because they claim to possess the truths of the church. Countermanding the impulses of Christians to claim superiority for— and exclusive rights to—the truths of their institutions and traditions, Tillich argues that "there is not freedom but demonic bondage where one's own truth is called the ultimate truth. For this [claim] is an attempt to be like God, an attempt which is made in the name of God."[20]

To countermand this tendency toward triumphalism, Tillich articulates and applies the Protestant principle, which is a critique directed toward oneself or one's perceptions and propositions. Simply, it recognizes that all human forms of reasoning and loving are imperfect, incomplete, and subject to ongoing, self-directed criticism because they are human and occur within the condition of estrangement from the ground of being. Because the expression of human freedom can take a perverted direction toward self-destruction, humans will always be in need of the Protestant principle. "The possibility of self-contradiction is rooted in the *self*-determination of man, the direction of which cannot be determined beforehand," Tillich notes. "This basic, underivable cleavage in human existence underlies all human history and makes history what it is."[21]

Although the Protestant principle protects one against the demonic assertion that one's experience and tradition constitute ultimate truth, it is still possible for one to experience assurance and joy in knowing eternal truth. For the nature of truth that frees the faithful who doubt is not, then, the truth of reasoned propositions, creedal affirmations, or logical derivations. The truth that liberates is an ontological truth, an experience of reality, of being itself. "If Jesus says, 'I am the truth,'" Tillich submits, "He indicates that in Him the true, the genuine, the ultimate reality is present; or, in other words, that God is present, unveiled, undistorted, in His infinite depth, in His unapproachable mystery." Clarifying the relation of truth to Jesus and his teachings, Tillich points out that "Jesus is not the truth because His teachings are true. But His teachings are true because they express the truth which He Himself is." They express the character of, and the reconciliation afforded by, the New Being that Jesus is as the Christ. The liberating function of truth, he continues, cannot be collapsed into the teaching of Jesus, despite mistaken efforts by devout Christians throughout history because "the words of Jesus, if taken as law, are not the truth which makes us free." Nor are the church's doctrines about Jesus the truth that sets the faithful free. Regrettably, Tillich bemoans, these assertions about the truth of doctrines, claimed as truth itself, have become tools "to prevent the honest search for truth—weapons to split the souls of people between loyalty to the Church and sincerity to truth."[22]

A genuine quest in faith—an honest search for the liberating truth revealed in the New Being of Jesus as the Christ—includes serious consideration and deliberation about whether one is of the truth. In other words, if doubt does not pertain in fundamental ways to one's experience in pursuit of truth, then truth cannot be perceived in reality. The person "who asks seriously the question of the truth that liberates is already on [the] way to liberation."[23] Liberating truth emerges from the struggle in existence as one wrestles toward the reconciliation that always exceeds the claim and always is present as a gift of New Being. Certainly, genuine seekers of truth, or "true doubters," will experience dimensions of the liberating power of truth even if they do not initially perceive it as such. A person may encounter liberating truth suddenly, in spectacular fashion, as with Paul's blinding illumination experience on the road to Damascus. Or, as Tillich indicates, one may encounter liberating truth gradually as "true reality appears like a landscape when the fog becomes thinner and thinner and finally disappears."[24] One may also encounter liberating truth in the beauty and temporality of nature or in an intense or intimate relationship with a friend.

Because "the truth which liberates is the power of love, for God is love," and because God is truth, Tillich cautions truth pursuers to be suspicious—to doubt every claim for truth that manifests no evidence of love. When estrangement is overcome in love, the truth and the reconciliatory power of Being (as revealed in the New Being of Christ) are not restricted to the recognition of revelation of New Being in Jesus as the Christ because the truth as love that liberates is ontological truth—the truth of being itself that undergirds, informs, and includes all reality. Such truth, Tillich concludes, "liberates from illusions and false authorities, from enslaving anxieties, desire and hostilities, from a wrong self-rejection and a wrong self-affirmation."[25] And such truth in love liberates Christians to enjoy the ecstatic experience of reunion with being itself in the frontier of faith.

Questions for Reflection

1. What becomes of spiritual certainty if Tillich is accurate about doubt being endemic to faith?

2. What becomes of absolute certainty of theological truth if Tillich is correct about the limits of truth?

3. What are the advantages of defining faith as "ultimate concern"?

THEOLOGY OF CULTURE

Religion is the substance of culture, culture is the form of religion.[1]

All arts create symbols for a level of reality which cannot be reached in any other way.[2]

Of course, theology cannot rest on scientific theory. But it must relate its understanding of man to an understanding of universal nature and statements about nature underlie every statement about him.[3]

Tillich's politics and his theology are of one foundation.[4]

From the earliest days of his theological career, Paul Tillich expressed fascination with the idea of culture and appreciation for its creative elements, especially the arts. His first published essay, "Uber die Idee einer Theologie der Kultur," challenged the traditional organization of theology that had relied on emphases such as apologetics, dogmatics, and ethics. Instead of replicating theology in these categories, at that time he suggested that "culture" supplant the category of ethics, and he insisted that the theology of culture should be extensive and pervasive, applying "not only to ethics but to all elements of culture."[5]

According to Tillich's vision, the first task of such a theology of culture is to provide "a general analysis of all cultural creations," and its starting point determines the significance of cultural creations and their "spiritual sustainability." Taking a second step, a theology of culture should set forth a typology of cultural creations from the perspective of their religious meaning, and at the same time it must provide a philosophy of cultural history. Tillich addresses this second task by proposing a threefold typology of culture—distinguishing autonomous, heteronomous, and theonomous forms—to use for classifying distinct cultural epochs throughout history. The final task for a theology of culture would be to sketch "the ideal outline of a culture penetrated by religion" while recognizing the shaping character of its own cultural perspective.[6]

This outline for a theonomous culture, however, does not actually create a culture itself; rather, the culture is produced by scientific principles and discoveries, legal statutes, moral acts, economic systems and exchanges, and artistic visions and works. In short, the sketch of a theonomous culture is embedded within the host culture of the theologian, who consciously uses its concepts and symbols in constructing the outline. In particular, the concepts and symbols of art, science, and politics provide the prompts and means for formulating the questions to which theology is then challenged to supply the response or answer.

In general, Tillich's understanding of the relation between religion and culture is based on his classification of three models of cultural orientation: autonomy, heteronomy, and theonomy. He defines an autonomous culture as one in which persons think that they possess universal reason and can determine their own laws. To a very real extent, the autonomous culture features humans assuming the role of God. Examples of periods when an autonomous form of culture prevailed are classical Greece, the Renaissance, the Enlightenment, and the European nineteenth century—all distinct epochs in Western civilizations. A heteronomous culture is one in which the religious expressions that had given rise to the culture have been made absolute, one in which attempts are made "to preserve and maintain a culture in terms of a particular moment in its creativity."[7] A heteronomous form of culture dominated the late Middle Ages and the eras of rigid Protestant orthodoxy. By contrast, Tillich determines that in a theonomous culture, persons realize that they are rooted in the ground of being, which transcends them by undergirding them. In a theonomous culture, which historically was prevalent during the High Middle Ages, persons' expressions also reveal their deepest values, their ultimate concern. Tillich notes, however, that there has never been—nor will there ever be—a pure expression of any of these ideal cultural forms, for all historical cultures have been mixtures of the autonomous, heteronomous, and theonomous forms. Consequently, he reasons that no cultural creation, whether it be one of an autonomous or heteronomous origin, can absolutely hide its religious ground in the admixture.

Thus, because "every finite reality is rooted in the creative ground, in Being itself," Tillich determines that the theonomous form of culture provides the standard for analyzing and evaluating the relations between culture and religion.[8] Recognizing this philosophical orientation, Tillich also observes that in the past two millennia, there has been a special historical relation between Christianity and culture, with Christianity providing the background for Western cultures. "No one living in the modern world," he declares, "can free himself from Christianity. It has permeated all the institutions and customs of modern society, as well as its moral and intellectual life."[9] While elements of Christianity pervade Western cultures, Western cultures also have affected all aspects of Christianity, Tillich avers, because Christianity is inconceivable apart from the linguistic structures, conceptual patterns, social groups, and public institutions that have contributed to its specific manifestations and development. Here Tillich identifies the specific application of his central dictum—that "religion is the substance of culture and culture the form of religion"—to Christianity. In this vein of thought he concludes that Christianity and culture are "within, not alongside each other" and that, therefore, "the kingdom of God includes both while transcending both."[10]

Even as Tillich moves from the larger theoretical consideration of relationship between religion and culture to indicate a special, historical relationship between Christianity and culture, he suggests a special relation of the Christian theologian to culture. As a part of the church, the Christian theologian can adopt any of three attitudes toward culture. The first, which typifies the perspective of many conservative Protestant ministers and thinkers, regards the world as being "over-against" the kingdom of God. This attitude annuls all possibilities for a genuine theology of culture since it presumes that culture contradicts, or is irrelevant to, the Christian message.

The second possible relation, which Tillich identifies with prominent mainline Protestant attitudes, is that both church and culture enjoy relative, partial freedom. In this approach, however, the consideration of culture is often subordinated to the power and privilege of the church in order to allow for the possibility of "supernatural revelation."

Tillich espouses a third position that includes both the task and the goal of contemporary and future Protestant theology. Here, the theologian establishes the distinction between religious potentiality (religious principle) and religious actuality (religious culture), assigning absolute character only to the religious principle. In turn, the theologian could not define it in "purely abstract terms" or link it concretely "to every fleeting fashion of cultural development." The theologian, however, must make every effort "to ensure the continuity of [the religious principle's] concrete religious standpoint."[11] This defining attitude, Tillich claims, provides the only possibility for a positive relation between a theology of culture and the theology of the church. With this understanding of the positive interaction between culture and religion, Tillich determines that a viable theology of culture must explore the depths of culture, plumbing the meaning of its artistic works, its scientific theories, its economic systems, and its political institutions.

Developing this positive point of contact between Protestantism and the secular as a particular aspect of culture, Tillich argues that Protestantism has "a passion for the secular" because the history of Protestantism evinces its continual fight against the tendency to isolate the holy and restrict it to one realm of churchly or cultural life. In effect, Protestantism encourages encounters with the holy in all places and all experiences of culture.[12] Another significant factor involved in Tillich's appropriation of a special relation between Protestantism and culture is his high regard for what he calls the Protestant principle. It prompts and facilitates "the dissolution of the antithesis of the sacred and the profane" in modern society, for Protestantism consistently opposes the possibility of the objectification of grace by "emphasizing the infinite distance between God and man."[13] In other words, the Protestant principle stresses the relative nature of all that exists, even the church and its doctrines. It reminds us that nothing is absolute except God alone. While the church often participates in cultural changes, at times even taking a leading role, the Protestant principle challenges the possible reification of both church and culture.

Tillich believes that the ultimate concerns of persons are expressed most revealingly in their cultural creations of visual arts, architecture, literature, and music; and he thinks that the arts always furnish "the most sensitive barometer of a spiritual climate."[14] In order for art to be considered authentically religious, he reasons, it must reveal the deep structure of Being; it must prompt and facilitate an encounter with ultimate reality. As such, authentically religious art does not have to use as its content the persons, events, and symbols that religious traditions have for ages regarded with great piety. Tillich even goes so far as to claim that

> it is possible to see in a still-life by Cézanne, an animal picture by Marc, a landscape by Schmidt-Rottluff, and an erotic picture by Nolde, the direct revelation of an absolute reality in these relative things. The world import, experienced in the artist's religious ecstasy, shines through the things; they have become "holy" objects.[15]

All subject matter thus becomes a possible vehicle for an artistic expression of the holy. The basis of this possibility lies, of course, in Tillich's concept of symbolic power, not in the sense that it incorporates special symbols or familiar figures into the content of the work (as is often the case in "bad art"), but in the sense that it expresses "a level of reality to which only the artistic creation has an approach."[16]

Nonetheless, a work of art need not avoid traditional religious subjects and symbols in order to express the depths of being that the style discloses. However, the subject matter of a work of art is not its most significant religious element or dimension. Instead, for Tillich, it is primarily through style that the artist expresses the meaning of an epoch, for style expresses the unconscious dimensions of an artist's wrestling with the question of ultimate meaning. With distinctive style, then, art can evoke a sense of the ultimate through its disruptive force—its potential to ignite the import of a work of art by bursting forth from the depths of its subject matter. In this way, it draws upon the reality that God—as being itself—is present throughout all realms of existence.

> If the idea of God includes ultimate reality, everything that expresses ultimate reality expresses God whether it intends to do so or not. And there is nothing that could be excluded from this possibility because everything that has being is an expression, however preliminary or transitory it may be, of being-itself, of ultimate reality.[17]

Throughout his career, Tillich devoted a great deal of attention to the evocative power of art, even confessing on one occasion that he had learned more from viewing the works of great modern artists who "broke through into the realm out of which symbols are born" than he had learned from reading theological tomes.[18] Nonetheless, he recognizes and celebrates the insights generated in other cultural arenas. Although artistic symbols and style can reveal "the character of a spiritual situation," he holds that scientific concepts and theories, for instance, must forgo the dynamism of symbols "in favor of objective adequacy." Even so, he concludes that "science is of greater importance in the rise of a spiritual situation, but [that] art is the more important for its apprehension."[19]

As Tillich conceives the natural sciences and religion, they do not, and cannot, interfere with one another because they are independent of one another. Religion, as he has famously avowed, is rooted in an encounter with the holy, the ground and mystery of life and meaning. As such, religion, or faith, confesses the meaning of existence. Although the sciences explore the structures of finite existence, they have distinctly different purposes.[20] It is no surprise that Tillich distinguishes sharply between the language of the sciences and that of religion, for "scientific language is predominantly calculating and detached and religious language is predominantly existential or involved."[21]

In principle, then, scientists as scientists cannot and should not speak about the *meaning* of the natural objects of their studies. Likewise, people of faith cannot and should not make statements of fact about events in the world of nature based on a "literal" reading of their sacred texts. In actual practice, however, Tillich chastises both scientists and theologians for violating these limits. On the one hand, scientists may step over into philosophy or theology with statements about the existence or nonexistence of God. They may also ideologically assert that scientific concepts and theories about the finite constitute the only legitimate knowledge. On the other hand, Tillich critiques ecclesial authorities who take the language of the Bible as legitimate to judge biological, psychological, or historical claims. For instance, he says, "when you take the symbols of 'creation' or as 'consummation'...concerning the beginning and the end of the world, and then calculate that the creation has happened six thousand years ago,...then you confuse the dimensions."[22] As he puts it elsewhere: "Theology...must leave to science the description of the whole of objects and their interdependence in nature and history, in man and his world."[23]

It would be a mistake, however, to conclude that Tillich had little interest in science. He not only admired the methods of science but also applauded the ongoing self-critique in science that leads to new insights and advanced theories.[24] Moreover, Tillich had a romantic attachment to nature that both refreshed and inspired him. Nature, for him, was a frequent medium for ecstatic encounters with spiritual depths. Perhaps the most significant contribution of nature to Tillich's theological system came through his appreciation of Schelling's philosophy of the structures of nature, both inorganic and organic, as interrelated dimensions of reality. The idea of the multidimensional unity of life that undergirds part 4 of *Systematic Theology*, "Life and the Spirit," bears witness to his indebtedness to the philosophy of nature.

Notwithstanding the new direction that Tillich takes in developing a theology of culture that features the arts and embraces the sciences, he still attends to matters of theological ethics in occasional works, such as one in which he distinguishes "moralisms" from morality in a theonomous culture.[25] His most comprehensive treatment of the relation between the moral and the religious is found in one of his final books, *Morality and Beyond*, which he dedicated to his close friend and ethicist Reinhold Niebuhr. In it, he grounds his theological ethics in the models of culture as autonomous, heteronomous, and theonomous.

Tillich's views on ethics are consistent with his basic distinction between essence and existence. Because humans are inchoately grounded in essential reality, they have a universal sense of living compatibly with absolute obligation. In this Kantian sense, then, Tillich accepts and argues that morality is an unconditional demand. Also like Kant, Tillich is reticent to define the duties to which we are obligated. Tillich claims, as he does with all finite actual enterprises, that all concrete ethical obligations, rules, principles, duties, and others are conditioned and relative, "dependent on the social and psychological constellation"[26] of times, places, events, and circumstances. He says, "While morality as the pure form of essential self-affirmation is absolute, the concrete systems of moral imperatives, the 'moralisms' are relative."[27] Thus, Tillich's ethical perspective is discussed in terms of an essential moral imperative and concrete moral maxims, rules, and laws, or moralisms.

Tillich finds two problems with ethical views that propound absolute obligation but, in reality, are limited to relative standards. Why? Because no absolute standards can be enunciated absolutely in the ambiguous situation of human existence. As a result, some people become absolute skeptics, allowing for no concrete standards. Others absolutize relative maxims heteronomously and become repressive fanatics, allowing for no ethics but their own. Tillich rejects both moral skepticism and ethical relativism, arguing for a morality that recognizes the limits of humans to interpret absolute demand in finite existence. He asks, "Can we point to something that transcends both graceless moralism and normless relativism in ethical theory and action?"[28]

Because humans are estranged from their essential nature, they confuse the limitations of positive ethics with absolute ethics. In other words, they turn contextual precepts into absolute precepts, accepting ethical maxims as absolute (divine) commands when, in fact, they are not. Any commands that stand against us, external to us, even if we believe God is their author, are to be resisted as strange. We face a situation in which we resent the law and the law giver, and at the same time, we become burdened with guilt because we become deceitfully proud ("I have kept *all* the commandments") or we are plunged into hopeless despair ("I cannot keep *any* commandment"). Thus, we become either absolutists or cynics.

Creative moral action emerges from this sense of false pride or loathing failure. In our autonomy we attempt to concretize the absolute in finite existence. Heteronomously, we turn finite, relative ethical claims into absolutes. We end up full of pride or despair. With no success within reach of our experience, we are driven to grace. Theonomously, the absolute imperative is an essential part of our being. A new theonomy, a loving grace, appears to overcome the conflict. Grace, which is the experience of accepting oneself, though unacceptable, unites the burden of guilt and the isolating estrangement of unacceptability. Grace offers forgiveness for our false vanity, and grace effects our becoming new beings, making us acceptable to ourselves and God. In this ecstatic state of redemption, or salvation, we are enabled to pursue just behavior through self-effacing love. We become justified, though unjust, by the grace of forgiveness and self-acceptance. As transformed selves, we become loving selves. Self-love, then, is the beginning of creative morality. In this sense, self-love is the actual acceptance of oneself even as one is accepted essentially despite being unacceptable. Self-love is not selfishness; it is, rather, self-acceptance and self-affirmation, enabling selfless action that is empowered to effect justice.

Love is the ground, power, and aim of justice, and it forms the ultimate principle of morality in its union with justice. Love, therefore, is the root of a theonomous ethic in four ways. Love is unconditional, working in every concrete situation for the reunion of the separated, and love transforms brittle legalisms—the calcification of moralism—by overcoming rigid authorities with the principle of freedom. Love also is the source of grace that forgives and renews. Further, love includes justice, leading to just relationships.[29]

As William Schweiker has noted, Tillich's view of morality is deeply theological, rooted in the appearance of a grace/acceptance that reunites the person with his or her self, with one's essential ground (God), and that enables reconciliation and reunion with others in the power of *agape*, or love.[30] Decidedly experiential and dispositional, Tillich's moral compass depends on the redeemed attitude of the individual. At the same time, Tillich is unable to provide specific guidance with regard to a body of ethical precepts, except to identify the motive (perhaps as a command) of *agape* for specific behaviors.[31]

Even as Tillich's personal ethics is oriented to the standard of a theonomous culture, so too his social ethics follows a similar pattern. Throughout his career in both

Germany and the United States, Tillich was vitally concerned for the welfare of human communities. His writings on society provide insight into his positions on politics and economics. In ways consistent with his theology of culture, theological principles and ethical norms underlie both his political and economic ideas, and his application of the Protestant principle to political platforms (and parties) and to economic models prevents them from becoming idolatrous.

Most important for Tillich's economic and political ideas is the principle of *agape*, or love, which, as we have seen, is the grounding datum for theonomous human behavior and activity. Because all living beings are networked by the polarity of essence and existence, they manifest an absolute obligation toward one another.

Central elements in his thinking about political matters are concepts and symbols related to democracy, socialism, faithful realism, the demonic, and *kairos*. Based on his consistent position that all human constructs are subject to distortion, he valued the balance of powers that democracies enjoin. His critique of unbalanced and illegitimate political power in his book *The Socialist Decision* led to his dismissal from the University of Frankfurt. His preference for democracy was enunciated in terms of the competing extremes of totalitarian absolutism and unbridled individualism. These options did not recognize the dignity of all and the balance of justice with freedom. While Tillich appreciated the images and aspirations of utopian communities, his realism mitigated those hopes.

Part and parcel with a free and just democratic society, Tillich espoused socialist economics wherein individuals should bear respected responsibility for other individuals in communities that valued justice for all. In this regard he was brutally critical of laissez-faire capitalism because of its inherent unjust outcomes.[32]

Tillich's democratic and socialistic leanings were grounded in his religious worldview, which was forged by his commitment to "faithful realism," an understanding of real-world situations in the light of ultimate realities. When the principle of *agape* is manifest in human communities, these experiences of love can be termed as times of *kairos*, or periods filled with essential meaning. By contrast, he determines that the destructive and "demonic" conditions in communities are those that pervert justice and thwart human flourishing.[33]

Although Tillich does not devote a volume or section of his *Systematic Theology* to his early proposal that a theology of culture supersede more traditional theological emphases such as ethics and dogmatics, he developed a vibrant theology of culture by evaluating the conditions in which he lived: the rise of socialism in Germany, the totalitarianism of the Nazi regime, the promise and threat of democratic ideals in the United States, the clarity of scientific theories about nature, and the evocative power of aesthetic works.

Questions for Reflection

1. How is religion the substance of culture?
2. Is a theonomous culture an ideal type, a divine demand, or a realization of the kingdom of God?
3. How can secular culture provide a vehicle for expressing divine reality?
4. Without being oriented to rules, how do ethics direct or interact with politics and economics?

CHAPTER TEN

ABIDING CONTRIBUTIONS

So there was a hunger for the big picture: What does it mean? How do we put it together into a story? Ultimately, everything's got to have a narrative.... And there was a need for people...to tell a story of what this could mean.[1]

It was long an axiom among Tillich scholars that Tillich's contribution to...religious thought was in systematic theology and studies in religion and culture.[2]

The question raised and the answer proposed in the first epigraph above restates, in an oblique fashion, the rhythm of Paul Tillich's method of correlation, that of question and response. At the same time, the epigraph that appeared in the journal *Seed: Science Is Culture* raises the kinds of ontological questions that Tillich posed. In its context, the "hunger for the big picture" pertains to questions about the origin and nature of the entire universe, as Tillich might put it—the nature of being. The proposed answer is in terms of "story," not fact, theory, or infallible propositions. Hauntingly similar to Tillich's theology, meaning is proposed in this evocative citation to be found in narratives and stories, not in cold facts and obtuse theories. Then in the words of venerable Tillich scholar John J. Carey, the second epigraph succinctly summarizes Tillich's focal concerns—systematic theological expositions about matters of ultimate concern and the central and irreducible presence of religious impulses in the life of culture. In short, these epigraphs point to three of Tillich's abiding contributions: his dialectical method of correlation that locates its ground and its goal in being; his thoroughgoing integration of theological concepts with one another; and his expansive engagement with and reflection upon culture.

A fourth aspect of Tillich's theological legacy grows out of his use of existential language with respect to God, religion, and faith. Tillich's recognition of God as ultimate, his definition of religion as what concerns one ultimately, and his concept of faith as the state of being ultimately concerned are intertwined contributions that further the prospect for understanding the meaningfulness of life. Concurrent with his persistent use of language of ultimacy to distinguish God, religion, and faith was his "reversal" of language of transcendence, which he understood as being deep rather than high, as being immanent rather than remote, as being the ground that empowers all that is rather than a force from above that might manipulate finite matters. In this regard, Tillich also connected with depth psychology's probing for inner self, for gestalts of human longing for ultimacy. For him, theological doctrines are not dicta of faith but evocative symbolic representations of the ways that the divine can be understood. For example, the resurrection, the incarnation, the Christ, and the Holy Spirit are not theological concepts or dogmas requiring affirmation beyond the limits of reason alone but are symbolic designations that open up human experience to the power and possibility of being. Even the word *God*, Tillich insists, is a symbol for the God beyond the word *God*. In this respect, as always, a theologian's use of contemporary language and ideas to render ultimate truth in finite forms is risky. Tillich was roundly criticized for abandoning traditional formulations and insights for the new wineskins of the contemporary. Nevertheless, the contribution of his enterprise is witnessed in the continuing relevance of his approach to thinking and doing theology. This enduring relevance is seen in the power of his sermons to continue to speak to contemporary readers.

A fifth advance derives from Tillich's comprehensive understanding of God and faith. His understanding liberates theology to be lived rather than to be relegated to a set of propositions merely requiring one's assent and obedience. This dynamic approach is manifest in his identification of faith as the state of being grasped by ultimate concern, and the energy of faith is intensified by including doubt as one of its constitutive elements—often determining its creative edge as the believer courses a journey of continuing questions and answers. The substance of faith (its Catholic element) is challenged and invigorated by continuing reflection (faith's Protestant principle).

Finally, to elaborate on Carey's identification of Tillich's remarkable contribution in the area of religion and culture, Tillich's fascination with expressions of ultimate concern was not confined to traditional spiritual matters but extended to all matters, everything in culture. By grounding all expressions and artifacts of culture in being itself, Tillich recognized and celebrated their sacramental potential, their ability to reveal hidden dimensions of being itself. Simply, Tillich initiated the extensive exploration of the spiritual dimension disclosed by secular rituals, institutions, and aesthetic works. In the half century since his death, theologians who have followed his lead have explored issues of ultimate significance and challenge as they have seriously engaged fiction and theater, film and television, visual arts and architecture, and politics and sports, to name a few of the fields wherein his promising ideas are being tilled.

These abiding contributions indicate several ways that Tillich served as a theological pioneer, exploring boundaries and traversing creatively between the territories of philosophy and theology, between faith and culture, between Christianity and Buddhism, between the academy and the public. He was a thinker who theorized about everything and who attempted to show what matters and why.

APPENDIX 1: LIFE AND CAREER

1886	Born, Starzeddel, Germany
1903	Mother dies
1904–1909	Studies at universities of Berlin, Tübingen, and Halle
1910	Receives Doctor of Philosophy degree, University of Breslau
1912	Receives Licentiate degree, University of Halle
	Ordained in the Evangelical Church of the Prussian Union
1914	Marries Margarethe Wever
1914–1918	Army chaplain, World War I
1919–1924	Privatdozent, University of Berlin
1920	Death of sister, Johanna
1921	Divorced from Margarethe Wever
1924	Marries Hannah Werner Gottschow
1924–1925	Associate Professor of Theology, University of Marburg
1925–1929	Professor of Philosophy and Religious Studies, Dresden Institute of Technology
1927–1929	Adjunct Professor of Systematic Theology, University of Leipzig
1929–1933	Professor of Philosophy, University of Frankfurt
1933	Dismissed by the government from University of Frankfurt
	Immigrates to the United States
1933-1937	Visiting Professor, Union Theological Seminary, New York
1937–1940	Associate Professor of Philosophical Theology, Union
1940–1955	Professor of Philosophical Theology, Union
1940	Becomes American citizen
1955–1962	University Professor, Harvard University
1962–1965	Nuveen Professor, Divinity School, University of Chicago
1965	Dies in Chicago
1966	Ashes interred at New Harmony, Indiana

APPENDIX 2: SELECTED PUBLISHED WORKS

1925	*The Religious Situation*
1932	*The Socialist Decision*
1936	*On the Boundary*
1948	*The Shaking of the Foundations*
	The Protestant Era
1951	*Systematic Theology*, volume 1
1952	*The Courage to Be*
1954	*Love, Power, and Justice*
1955	*The New Being*
1956	*The Religious Situation*
1957	*Systematic Theology*, volume 2
	The Dynamics of Faith
1963	*Systematic Theology*, volume 3
	The Eternal Now
1965	*Theology of Culture*
1966	*On the Boundary: An Autobiographical Sketch*
1967	*My Search for Absolutes*

APPENDIX 3: LEXICON

Paul Tillich believed that the words of the theologian should be words that speak to the current situation. The theologian or preacher could not simply repeat or rehash "the faith once delivered," relying on ancient creedal formulae, an authorized biblical text such as the Elizabethan English of the King James Version, or the statements of theological icons such as Augustine, Thomas Aquinas, Luther, and Calvin. He said that holy language constitutes a legalism of the word (cited in James Luther Adams, *Paul Tillich's Philosophy of Culture, Science, and Religion* [New York: Schocken Books, 1965], 3).

In this appendix we provide a lexicon of salient words and phrases used by Tillich. Some of them, such as *ultimate concern*, *the ground of being*, and *the New Being*, are signature concepts of Tillich's theology. Other, more familiar terms, such as *faith*, *doubt*, and *spirit*, have particular Tillichean nuances. Thus, a "vocabulary lesson" will advance one's understanding of what initially may appear opaque, on the one hand, or mundane, on the other. We have organized these brief definitions of key terms alphabetically. Use the index to track these entries in the text.

Alienation. A consequence of existence; it is the condition of sin. See "Estrangement," which is the term Tillich preferred.

Ambiguity. The condition of everything in life that mixes the essential with finite existence. The ontological structures of being are, in existence, threatened by nonbeing, thereby resulting in ambiguity in every aspect of life, including the lack of certain meaning, truth, and value (*ST*, 3:162–282). See "Despair."

Anxiety. Anxiety is "finitude in awareness" (*ST*, 1:191). Although it might be latent, anxiety is an ontological quality that is omnipresent as a characteristic of existence. It is independent of any object through which its threat might be perceived, but it is present wherever there is the threat of nonbeing. Anxiety is overcome in the process of reconciliation when that which has been estranged is reunited with its essence.

Apologetic Theology. Apologetic theology, with which Tillich identifies, seeks to answer "the questions implied in the [contemporary] situation in the power of the eternal message . . . with the means provided by the situation whose questions it answers" (*ST*, 1:6). While apologetic theology seeks to make the eternal message relevant to the current situation, it must seek not to lose the essential truth in current language. It seeks a method "in which message and situation are related in such a way that neither of them is obliterated" (*ST*, 1:8). It uses the "principle of correlation" as a guide.

Autonomy. In autonomy (*auto* [self] + *nomos* [law]) a person self-rules, affirming and actualizing the structure of reason without regard to reason's theonomous roots. In autonomy a person obeys his or her own reasoning capabilities but without acknowledging that the structures of reason are rooted in the ground of being (*ST*, 1:83–84).

Being. The source and power for all that exists. Being is the ground from which all that exists gets its power to exist. Being includes all that is, and being is so comprehensive that it includes within itself the very threat of its annihilation, non-being (*me on*).

Being Grasped. The state of ultimate concern where "he who is grasped and that by which he is grasped are ... at the same place." One "participates" in the object of one's ultimate concern, however inchoately (*DF*, 99).

Border Situation. Sometimes used as a synonym for boundary situation. It also may refer to the existential experience of living on the border between two entities or forces, such as two cultures or two philosophies, or dimensions. Tillich refers to these experiences as standing between alternative possibilities of existence. See *OB*.

Boundary Situation. All finite entities exist at the boundary of being and nonbeing. Therefore, decisions about what to think and do include both a free autonomous and creative element and a fated and possibly destructive component. Although persons frequently deceive themselves by retreating to the security of ideology or dogma, they remain in the anxiety of nonbeing.

Catholic Substance. The notion of Catholic substance is correlative to the Protestant principle in the sense that affirmations about God have a divine content, or substance. Christian faith, for example, makes claims about God, Christ, salvation, eternal life, the kingdom, and so on. These universals (Tillich prefers to call them symbols) are shared by all Christians. Concrete claims about these symbols (the core of doctrines) are subject to critique based on the Protestant principle.

Correlation. A key to understanding Tillich's thought, correlation is his theological method, which "explains the contents of the Christian faith through existential questions and theological answers in mutual interdependence" (*ST*, 1:60). This approach is necessary because theology must be apologetic, answering the questions of existence with the truths of revelation. "The answers implied in the event of revelation are meaningful only in so far as they are in correlation with questions concerning the whole of our existence, with existential questions" (*ST*, 1:61).

Courage. Courage is an ontological concept that gives rise to an ethical reality. As such, it enjoys a reciprocal relation with being, for "courage can show us what being is, and being can show us what courage is" (*CB*, 2). Empowered by being, courage generates moral action, and it "is the key to being-itself" (*CB*, 181).

The Courage to Be. Finite existence, fraught with sin, fate, guilt, emptiness, and angst—all which threaten one's being—is burdened by fear. Through faith, one is able to "be" and to live in hope and love, regardless of the threats of existence. See *CB*.

Creation/Creator. God is the maker of heaven and earth. Creative action is a central action of God. "The divine life is creative"; "The doctrine of creation is not the story of an event" that took place in history (*ST*, 1:252). The theological sense of God as creator is that all (heaven and earth) depends on God. The creation is therefore rooted in God's creativity.

Culture. Culture is the form of religion. It is the vehicle through which "ultimate concern" can be expressed. It is the totality of symbols expressed through language, the arts, science, politics, and philosophy. Because religion provides "the meaning-giving substance to culture," one can discern "the basic concern of religion" throughout the expressions of culture (*TC*, 42).

The Demonic. This is neither the devil nor a gaggle of demons that are personal, spiritual beings who taunt and tempt. Rather, the demonic is the inclination and act that "distorts self-transcendence by identifying a particular bearer of holiness with the holy itself" (ST, 3:102).

Depth. The innermost spiritual reality that is symbolically "beneath" finite existence.

Despair. The state of conflict in ambiguous existence that leads to hopelessness and even suicide. Also, despair is the agony of being responsible for one's estrangement and separation from meaning, truth, and life, including the inability to overcome it (ST, 2:75–78).

Dimensions. A spatial metaphor favored by Tillich to refer to the unity of life and its functions—morality, culture, and religion. As dimensions, they do not interfere with one another, and yet they intersect at one point that enables them to be a multidimensional unity (ST, 3:15). *Realm* and *gradation* are correlative terms (see ST, 3:16–17).

Doubt. Tillich's definition of faith implies that one's submission to a "perceived ultimate" may be a commitment to a false god (or gods). One's faith is finite, and therefore faith commitments are finite, even though one intends to connect to the ultimate. Thus, one's commitment is fraught with ambiguity. Commitments can "miss the mark," be distorted, erroneous, or mistaken. People of faith cannot be certain that they have committed to the unconditional ground of being. Faith includes an element of intellectual and emotional doubt. One can be uncertain of beliefs about the object of one's commitment and anxious about the validity of one's faith. Doubt is not the result of a deficient faith; however, it is a creative, urging edge of faith. Not denial but wonder. See *DF*, especially 16–22.

Dreaming Innocence. Tillich rejects the historic fall of human beings from a state of sinlessness and immortality to a state of disobedience and finite death. He suggests "a kind of dreaming innocence, a stage of infancy before contest and decision" (ST, 1:259). Dreaming innocence reflects the human desire to preserve the mythic, Edenic harmony between freedom and destiny. Dreaming innocence "precedes actual existence. It has potentiality, not actuality" (ST, 2:35). It is a state of mind. Usually, these "dreamers" live in the refusal of their estrangement, often uncritically following the idols of dogma and tyranny. The dreamers are not actually "living" because they are innocent of the necessity to engage the ambiguities of life.

Ecstasy. The state of being grasped by Spiritual Presence, making the unambiguous life possible. See *DF*, 6–8.

Essence/Existence. Essence is being as such. It is the pure form of being, the intention of creation itself. Essence is the power of being that resides in all that is. In existence, essence cannot be fully actualized because existence is constrained by the finitude of time, space, and human reason.

Estrangement/Alienation. Estrangement is the separation of existence from essence, of the estranged being from its essence. Because separation occurs with existence, it is the human predicament. The "first mark" of estrangement is this disconnection from one's essence; it includes "unbelief" and "un-love" (ST, 2:49). The goal of salvation is reunion with essence, for New Being is the "reality in which the self-estrangement of our existence is overcome, a reality of reconciliation and reunion, of creativity, meaning and hope" (ST, 1:49).

Eternal Life/Eternal Now. Tillich questions classic notions of life after death. He rejects the idea of endless linear time (*chronos*) in another dimension. Neither does he, like many modern theologians, believe in a "soul," or spiritual essence that survives death. For Tillich, eternal life is not the "continuation of the temporal life of an individual after death without a body" (*ST*, 3:409). If, in salvation, one is grasped by the eternal, returning to whence one has come, life in the eternal is affirmed. Tillich emphasizes the present love that alleviates the anxiety over one's finitude, providing courage for living fully in the present. The eternal is "now" when we are grasped by it. Eternity is "a quality that transcends temporality" (*ST*, 3:410). He does not reject self-conscious existence after death, but neither does he affirm it (*ST*, 3:414).

Existential. "Existential is what characterizes our real existence in all its concreteness, in all its accidental elements, in its freedom and responsibility, in its failure, and in its separation from its true and essential being" (Tillich, "Philosophy and Theology," *Religion in Life* 10 [1941]: 28).

Faith. Faith is the state of being ultimately concerned. As a centered act of the total person, it includes one's volitional, intellectual, physical, and emotional states. One's entire self surrenders and submits to that which one perceives as the ultimate and unconditioned. Tillich says, "Faith is not an opinion but a state. It is the state of being grasped by the power of being" (*CB*, 173; see also *DF*, 1–35).

Fall. Like the doctrine of creation, the fall of humanity is not a story from history. Humanity, in a dual existence, is separated from its essential relatedness to God. The freedom that humanity exercises in existence implies that humans are "outside" the divine life. The fall is a symbol for the human condition universally (see *ST*, 1:252–56, and *ST*, 2:29–44). It is the universal condition of being "in sin," that is, separated from one's essential self, God, and others.

Gestalt of Grace. The structure of faith. According to Tillich, in the experience of faith,

> We are justified by grace *alone*, because in our relation to God we are dependent on God, on God alone, and in no way on ourselves; we are grasped by grace, and this is only another way of saying that we have faith. Grace creates the faith through which it is received. Man does not create faith by will or intellect or emotional self-surrender. Grace comes to him; it is "objective," and he may be enabled to receive it, or he may not. (*TPE*, xvii)

God. God is the name for that which concerns one ultimately. Whatever is of ultimate concern therefore becomes one's god (*ST*, 1:211). God (with a capital G) is the absolute, essential, unconditioned ground of concrete reality, or what is; that is, the ground of being. Since knowledge of God is always conditioned by culture and context, and therefore not absolute, Tillich refers to the absolute as "the God beyond God." See the following entry, "God beyond God."

God beyond God. The "God above God" is the "God beyond God," the absolute God beyond the inherent ambiguity of all human concepts of God. The absolute God is "present, although hidden, in every divine-human encounter" (*CB*, 190–93).

Grace. "Grace is the reunion of life with life, the reconciliation of the self with itself.

Grace is the acceptance of that which is rejected. Grace transforms fate into a meaningful destiny; it changes guilt into confidence and courage. There is something triumphant in the word 'grace': in spite of the abounding of sin grace abounds much more" (*SF*, 156).

Heteronomy. Heteronomy is the imposition of a strange (*heteros*) law (*nomos*) on one or more of the functions of reason. "The problem of heteronomy is the problem of an authority which claims to represent reasons . . . against its autonomous actualization" (*ST*, 1:84). Heteronomous reason appears as a false theonomy. Heteronomy usually arises when autonomy has lost its depth (*ST*, 1:85).

The Holy. The "greatness" of the religious dimension. The manifestation of the divine ground of being within anything (person, rite, word, cultural creation) in finite existence. Holiness refers to the power of pointing beyond to the essential ground. The profanization of the holy is one ambiguity of religion (*ST*, 3:98–100).

Idolatry. Idolatry is a commitment to a false god (or gods). The object/s of these mistakes is/are idols. Any concrete entity (e.g., nation, ideology, religious institution, pleasure, happiness, success, etc.) qualifies as a potential false god. Idolatrous faith mistakes the conditional for the unconditional; the finite for the infinite (see *DF*, 12–16).

Jesus as the Christ. Tillich distinguishes between the "historical Jesus" and "the Christ of faith," also specified as "Jesus as the Christ." The former is the Jesus of history; the latter, the savior or deliverer, the reconciler of God and humanity. In his own words, Tillich indicates that

> Jesus as the Christ is the bearer of the New Being in the totality of his being, not in any special expressions of it. It is his being that makes him the Christ because his being has the quality of the New Being beyond the split of essential and existential being. From this it follows that neither his words, deeds, or sufferings nor what is called his "inner life" make him the Christ. They are all expressions of the New Being, which is the quality of his being, and this, his being, precedes and transcends all its expressions. (*ST*, 2:121)

Justice. The true power of being. The unconditional command that others (thous) be accorded the same dignity as the self (the *I*). (See *LPJ*, 54-71.)

Kairos. By *kairos*, Tillich refers to the times in mundane history (where time is *chronos*) in which the *Logos*—the universal and unconditional truth—is manifest in existence. *Kairos* is not "a time, but rather 'the right time,' the moment rich in content and significance" (Tillich, *kairos*, *TPE*, 33). Kairotic moments (or periods, or ages) are theonomous, that is, in them the meaning, mystery, and divine significance of all cultural forms and functions are manifest, or possibly manifest (*TPE*, 43–44). The mystical ecstasy of *kairos* has a correlate in autonomous reason. Human reason explicates kairotic moments, giving them historical meanings and purpose. All of human cultural activity is based on this dynamic element. The polarity of theonomy and autonomy "is that in an autonomous culture the cultural forms appear only in their finite relationship, while in a theonomous culture they appear in the relation to the unconditional" (*TPE*, 45). Threatening this polar relationship is heteronomy, the situation in culture when either the religious impulse of theonomy or the secular orientation of autonomony becomes dominant. Either a religious or a secular tyranny results, destroying *kairos* and replacing it with either absolutist religions or totalitarian states.

Kerygmatic Theology. Kerygmatic theology emphasizes traditional concepts and solutions, often receiving as eternal truth dogmas, creeds, and theologies of the past as unchanging truths. These theologies confuse eternal truth with temporal expressions of this truth. Tillich cites orthodoxies, fundamentalisms, and the neo-Reformation theology of Karl Barth as expressions of kerygmatic theology (*ST*, 1:4–8).

Latent Church/Manifest Church. Communities not formally associated with "manifest" (actual) churches that, nonetheless, participate tacitly in the ultimate concern that drives the actual churches, although their perceptions of ultimacy are muted by culture and ignorance (see *ST*, 3:152–55).

Life. The actuality of being. Essential life refers to the potential to become actual, in existence, as actualized life becomes subjected to finitude, estrangement, and the threat of death. Life, then, is a mixture of essential and existential elements. Life is therefore multidimensional (see *ST*, 3:11–12).

Love. Love is the power of the ground of being. Love drives one toward a reunion with the ultimate and with the ground itself from which it is separated. Love is the means by which our separation from God, others, and ourselves is overcome. Love is the essence of life itself. "Love lasts, love alone endures, and nothing else besides love, nothing independent of love." Love enables reconciliation, forgiveness, and reunion, and love alleviates our fear of nonbeing (see *DF*, 112–17).

Miracles. Miracles are not happenings that contradict the laws of nature. Nor is a miracle "a supranatural interference which destroys the natural structure of events" (*ST*, 1:115). Miracles, rather, are "sign-events" in which being is manifest in human existence. Miracles "shock" the mind into affirming the presence of God in existence (see *ST*, 1:115–18).

Myth. Myth has multiple definitions in modern thought. For Tillich, myth is an important component of religious language. Myths are action stories of God (or the gods) with human beings in time and space. They can be taken as "actual" events, but in theology, myths are understood not literally or historically, but symbolically. Tillich rejects the notion that the creation narratives, the virgin birth, and the ascension are historical; nevertheless, they are rich with symbolic meanings of ultimate import (see *DF*, 55–62).

New Being. Jesus as the Christ is the manifestation of God (essential Being) in existence. He is the revealer of a new reality, a new creation, a new state of things. As uniquely manifested in Jesus as the Christ, the New Being is the return to and the reemergence of the unity life in love. In existence, life is broken, distorted, split from its essential self. The New Being is a renewal and return to an undivided self. It is characterized by reconciliation, reunion, and resurrection. Participating in the New Being (see 2 Cor. 5:17—"in Christ") is the promise and proclamation of Christianity (see Tillich's sermon "The New Being" in the volume of sermons of the same title, 15–24).

Nonbeing. Nonbeing is a threat to life and the chief problem of existence. But the reality of the threat of nonbeing means that it must be embraced within the power of being itself. Consequently, Tillich says, being cannot be considered alone; it must be seen in dialectical relation with nonbeing, which is present as a threat wherever there is being. And "where there is nonbeing," Tillich concludes, "there is finitude and anxiety" (CB, 180).

Ontological Elements. The essential structures of reality that are qualities of everything. These elements—individualization and participation, dynamics and form, and freedom and destiny—are in polar relationships with one another (see ST, 1:174–86).

Ontology. Ontology "is an analysis of those structures of being which we encounter in every meeting with reality" (ST, 1:20). In Tillich's usage the discipline of philosophy asks the question of the structure of being. Theology asks, but from a different perspective, the same question in the sense that our ultimate concern must belong to what "is." Every theological statement therefore presupposes the categories, laws, and concepts of the structure of being (ST, 1:21–23).

Pantheism/Panentheism. Pantheism is the conflated identity of God with nature or, variously, the divinization of nature. Although some critics claim that Tillich's notion of God as the Unconditioned or as Being is compatible with pantheism, Tillich denies this charge. His position is more in line with panentheism, the view that God is present in all that is, but that all that is does not constitute the fullness of God. While God is "the one in whom we live and move and have our being," God exceeds infinitely all that is. Tillich says, "God is immanent in the world as its permanent creative ground and is transcendent to the world through freedom" (ST, 1:263). Following Rudolf Otto, Tillich claims that the presence of God's holiness transcends the subject-object structure of reality (ST, 1:215–16).

Participation. See "Being Grasped."

Power. A dynamic force urged by love. Power "drives the human spirit above itself towards what it cannot attain by itself, the love that is greater than all other gifts, the truth in which the depth of being opens itself to us, the holy that is the manifestation of the presence of the ultimate" ("Spiritual Presence," in EN, 84).

Protestant Principle. The Protestant principle is not Tillich's attempt to specify the core affirmation of the Protestant churches. Rather, it refers to the possibility that every theological statement (e.g., that God is infinite, omniscient, personal, and so on) may be questioned, critically assessed, and reformulated. No book, no religious authority, no creedal traditions, no confessions of truth, in fact, no human claims to truth, are absolute. All theological claims remain subject to reform. According to Tillich, the Protestant principle "is the critical element in the expression of the community of faith and consequently the element of doubt in the act of faith" (DF, 29).

Providence. Providence is God's sustaining creativity. It "is not a theory about some activities of God; it is the religious symbol of the courage of confidence with respect to fate and death" (CB, 168–69). In and through the fatedness and freedom of human existence, God is "with us" essentially. Although ambiguity and anxiety beset every human experience, Tillich claims that the person "who believes in providence does not believe that a special divine activity will alter the conditions of finitude and estrangement. He believes and asserts with the courage of faith, that no situation whatsoever can frustrate the fulfillment of his ultimate destiny" (ST, 1:267; Tillich references Rom. 8:31-38).

Reason. Tillich distinguishes between ontological reason and technical reason. In the former, reason is the meaning structure of both mind and reality/being. In the latter, reason is the process of thinking scientifically, by the logics of deduction and induction. Ontological reason is a precondition for faith because in faith, reason reaches ecstatically beyond itself, grasping (and being grasped by) ultimate truth, unconditional commands, and the presence of the holy (see *DF*, 85–91).

Religion. Religion is "the self-transcendence of life under the dimension of spirit" (*ST*, 3:96). Religion is inherently ambiguous in finite existence. Through its rites and teachings, it becomes a vehicle of the holy, but at the same time, it has the tendency to transform vehicles of the holy into a finite object among finite objects. It thereby profanes the holy (*ST*, 3:98). "The profanization of religion has the character of transforming it into a finite object among finite objects" (*ST*, 3:98). In its holy function as medium of the message, religion also demonizes the self-transcendent experience "by identifying a particular bearer of holiness with the holy itself" (*ST*, 3:102).

Revelation. Revelation is not information received about divine matters in words. It is not "propositional." Rather, revelation is an "experience in which an ultimate concern grasps the human mind and creates a community in which this concern expresses itself in symbols of action, imagination, and thought" (*DF*, 78).

Salvation. Salvation refers to a multidirected experience that is mediated by Jesus as the Christ in which a person is rescued or freed from ultimate negativity and at the same time returned to a centered self in relation to God, self, and others (see *ST*, 2:165–68, and 3:277–82).

Separation. See "Sin" and "Alienation."

Sin. For Tillich, sin is the state of separation (alienation, estrangement) of humans from God. One is therefore alienated from oneself and others. Sins are "personal act[s] of turning away from that to which one [essentially] belongs" (see *ST*, 2:165–67). All persons are in the state of sin; thus, all are "fallen." Sin is a human state or condition; sins are behaviors resulting from being in the condition of sin. Sins result from being disunified from God, self, and others. Love, as "the striving for the reunion of the separated," conquers sin (*ST*, 2:44–47).

Spirit/spirit. A dimension of life that unites the power of being (Spirit) with the meaning of being (Spirit). The actualization of power and meaning in unity (*ST*, 3:111). Makes possible human awareness of self-transcendence and the possibility of being grasped by Spiritual Presence.

Spiritual Community. The church in its essence; also called the community of faith. The life of faith is lived out in a community of believers who manifest the love of God to one another and to others (see *DF*, 117–19).

Spiritual Presence. An alternative term to *Holy Spirit* or *spirit of God*. The experience of the power of being in a renewed state of being. The result of overcoming sin in salvation by the power of love. It is "a power that is in us but not of us, qualifying for the service of a new state of things" (see "Spiritual Presence," in *EN*, 81–91).

Symbol. Symbol, along with myth, is the peculiar language of faith that intends to express truth about ultimacy in words. Key symbols, such as God, being, existence, life, love, and power, are like pictures or poems, pointing beyond themselves to disclose a reality that cannot be expressed in ordinary discourse. Symbols also "participate" in the realities to which they point, opening up dimensions of reality and essential aspects of ourselves. The symbol God, for example, "points beyond itself while participating in that to which it points" (see *DF*, 47–55).

Theism. The "God above God" more specifically refers to the God above the God of "theological theism" or, more commonly, "the God of theism." The God of theism is a theological construct, not the ultimate. The theistic God is "a being" and not "being itself." As "a being," the theistic God is existent and is characterized in "personal" terms. The God above God does not exist, but is the absolute ground of all that exists. Contrary to some, Tillich's claim that the God of theism does "not exist" as the ultimate or ground of being has no defining content. He means rather that the historic claims about God (often referred to as "historic theism") are finite, and these tentative claims are subject to critique (doubt) and to reconception. Therefore he can write, "God does not exist. He is being-itself, beyond essence and existence. Therefore, to claim that God exists is to deny him" (*ST*, 1:205).

Theology. Theology is "the statement of the truth of the Christian message and the interpretation of this truth of every new generation." As such, theology operates on a continuum of two poles, one with reference to the past ("the eternal truth of its foundation") and one with reference to the present ("the temporal situation in which the eternal truth must be received") (*ST*, 1:3). "The task of theology . . . is mediation between the eternal criterion of truth as it is manifest in the picture of Jesus as the Christ and the changing experiences of individuals and groups, their varying questions, and their categories of perceiving reality" (*TPE*, ix). See "Apologetic Theology" and "Kerygmatic Theology" for two alternatives to mediating between the eternal truth (*theos*) and the contemporary situation (*logos*).

Theonomy. Theonomy (*theos* [God] + *nomos* [law]) is the condition of being ruled by God. More specifically in Tillich's use, it refers to the depth of reason in its essence. In a theonomous situation, law and reason, form and substance, are unified because both are grounded in God. In existence, however, there can be no complete theonomy because the limits of finitude confine existents in time and place and constrict the perfection of reason (*ST*, 1:85).

Ultimate. Tillich distinguishes between "The Ultimate" and one's "perceived ultimate." The former designates the essential ground of being, or the unconditioned, which transcends every finite faith commitment. The latter refers to that which one freely chooses as the object of one's faith. The object of one's concrete faith is thus in tension between the "perceived ultimate" and the "essential Ultimate."

The Word of God. "Any reality by means of which the eternal breaks with unconditional power into our contemporaneity" (cited by J. L. Adams from Tillich's *Religiöse Veriverklichung* [Berlin: Furche, 1930], 85).

BIBLIOGRAPHY

I. Major Works of Paul Tillich

Biblical Religion and the Search for Ultimate Reality. Chicago: University of Chicago Press, 1955.

Christianity and the Encounter of the World Religions. New York: Columbia University Press, 1963.

The Construction of the History of Religion in Schelling's Positive Philosophy: Its Presuppositions and Principles. Translated by Victor Nuovo. Lewisburg, Pa.: Bucknell University Press, 1974.

The Courage to Be. New Haven: Yale University Press, 1952.

The Dynamics of Faith. New York: Harper & Row, 1957.

The Eternal Now. New York: Charles Scribner's Sons, 1963.

The Future of Religions. Edited by Jerald C. Brauer. New York: Harper & Row, 1966.

A History of Christian Thought: From Its Judaic and Hellenistic Origins to Existentialism. Edited by Carl E. Braaten. New York: Simon and Schuster, 1967.

The Interpretation of History. Translated by N. A. Rasetski and Elsa L. Talmey. New York: Charles Scribner's Sons, 1936.

The Irrelevance and Relevance of the Christian Message. Edited by Durwood Foster. Cleveland: Pilgrim Press, 1996.

Love, Power, and Justice. New York: Oxford University Press, 1954.

Morality and Beyond. New York: Charles Scribner's Sons, 1963. Reprinted with a foreword by William Schweiker. Louisville: Westminster John Knox Press, 1995.

My Search for Absolutes. New York: Simon and Schuster, 1967.

My Travel Diary—1936: Between Two Worlds. Edited and with an introduction by Jerald C. Brauer. Translated by Maria Pelikan. New York: Harper & Row, 1970.

Mysticism and Guilt-Consciousness in Schelling's Philosophical Development. Translated by Victor Nuovo. Lewisburg, Pa.: Bucknell University Press, 1974.

The New Being. New York: Charles Scribner's Sons, 1955.

On Art and Architecture. Edited by John Dillenberger and Jane Dillenberger. New York: Crossroad, 1987.

On the Boundary: An Autobiographical Sketch. New York: Charles Scribner's Sons, 1966.

Political Expectation. Edited and with an introduction by James Luther Adams. New York: Harper & Row, 1971.

The Protestant Era. Translated by James Luther Adams. Chicago: University of Chicago Press, 1948.

The Religious Situation. Translated by H. Richard Niebuhr. New York: Meridian Books, 1956.

The Shaking of the Foundations. New York: Charles Scribner's Sons, 1948.

The Socialist Decision. Translated by Franklin Sherman. New York: Harper & Row, 1977.

The Spiritual Situation in Our Technical Society. Edited by J. Mark Thomas. Macon, Ga.: Mercer University Press, 1988.

Systematic Theology. 3 vols. Chicago: University of Chicago Press, 1951, 1957, 1963.

Theology of Culture. Edited by Robert C. Kimball. New York: Oxford University Press, 1959, 1964.

Ultimate Concern: Tillich in Dialogue. Edited by D. MacKenzie Brown. New York: Evanston, 1956.

What Is Religion? Edited and with an introduction by James Luther Adams. New York: Harper & Row, 1969.

II. Selected Essays and Articles of Paul Tillich

"Contemporary Protestant Architecture." Pages 122–25 in *Modern Church Architecture*. Edited by Albert Christ-Janer and Mary Mix Foley. New York: McGraw-Hill, 1962. (Also included in *On Art and Architecture*.)

"Existentialist Aspects of Modern Art." Pages 128–47 in *Christianity and the Existentialists*. Edited by Carl Michalson. New York: Charles Scribner's Sons, 1956. (Also included in *On Art and Architecture*.)

"The Meaning and Justification of Religious Symbols." Pages 3–11 in *Religious Experience and Truth*. Edited by Sydney Hook. New York: New York University Press, 1961.

The Meaning of Health: Essays in Existentialism, Psychoanalysis, and Religion. Edited by Perry LeFevre. Chicago: Exploration Press, 1984.

"The Nature of Religious Art," with Theodore M. Greene. *Symbols and Society*. Edited by Lyman Bryson et al. New York: Harper Brothers, 1955.

"Reinhold Niebuhr's Doctrine of Knowledge." *Reinhold Niebuhr: His Religious, Social, and Political Thought*. Edited by Charles W. Kegley and Robert W. Bretall. New York: Macmillan, 1956.

"Sin and Grace in the Theology of Reinhold Niebuhr." *Reinhold Niebuhr: A Prophetic Voice in Our Time*. Edited by Harold R. Landon. Greenwich, Conn.: Seabury Press, 1962.

"Symbols of Eternal Life." *Harvard Divinity Bulletin* 26 (April 1962):1–10.

"Theology and Symbolism." Pages 107–16 in *Religious Symbolism*. Edited by F. Ernest Johnson. New York: Harper and Brothers, 1955.

"The Two Types of Philosophy of Religion." *Union Seminary Quarterly Review* I (May 1946): 3–13.

"The World Situation." *The Christian Answer*. Edited by Henry P. Van Dusen. New York: Charles Scribner's Sons, 1945. (Also Philadelphia: Fortress Press, 1965.)

III. Selected Studies on Paul Tillich

Adams, James Luther. *Paul Tillich's Philosophy of Culture, Science, and Religion*. New York: Harper & Row, 1965.

Adams, J. L., W. Pauck, and R. L. Shinn, eds. *The Thought of Paul Tillich*. San Francisco: Harper & Row, 1985.

Board, Rachael Sophia. "Original Grace, Not Destructive Grace: A Feminist Appropriation of Paul Tillich's Notion of Acceptance." *Journal of Religion* 87 (July 2007): 411–34.

Bulman, Raymond F. *A Blueprint for Humanity: Paul Tillich's Theology of Culture*. East Brunswick, N.J.: Associated University Presses, 1981.

Bulman, Raymond F., and Frederick J. Parrella. *Paul Tillich: A New Catholic Assessment*. New York: Health Policy Advisory Center, 1994.

Carey, John J., ed. *Kairos and Logos: Studies in the Roots and Implications of Tillich's Theology*. Cambridge, Mass.: North American Paul Tillich Society, 1978.

———, ed. *Theonomy and Autonomy: Studies in Paul Tillich's Engagements with Modern Culture*. Macon, Ga.: Mercer University Press, 1984.

———. *Tillich Studies: 1975*. Tallahassee: North American Paul Tillich Society, 1975.

Clayton, John Powell. *The Concept of Correlation: Paul Tillich and the Possibility of a Mediating Theology*. Berlin: Walter de Gruyter, 1980.

Dourley, John P. *Paul Tillich, Carl Jung, and the Recovery of Religion*. London: Routledge, 2008.

Drummy, Michael F. *Being and Earth: Paul Tillich's Theology of Nature*. New York: University Press of America, 2000.

Gilkey, Langdon. *Gilkey on Tillich*. New York: Crossroad, 1990.

———. "The Symbol of God." *Soundings* 69 (Winter 1986): 384–400.

Hammond, Guyton B. *Man in Estrangement: A Comparison of the Thought of Paul Tillich and Erich Fromm*. Nashville: Vanderbilt University Press, 1965.

———. *The Power of Self-Transcendence: An Introduction to the Philosophical Theology of Paul Tillich*. St. Louis: Bethany Press, 1966.

Kegley, Charles W., and Robert W. Bretall, eds. *The Theology of Paul Tillich*. New York: Macmillan, 1952, 1961, 1964; New York: Pilgrim Press, 1982.

Kelsey, David. *The Fabric of Paul Tillich's Theology*. New Haven: Yale University Press, 1967.

Lichtman, Susan. "The Concept of Sin in the Theology of Paul Tillich: A Break from Patriarchy." *Journal of Women and Religion* 8 (Winter 1989): 49–55.

Manning, Russell, ed. *The Cambridge Companion to Paul Tillich*. Cambridge: Cambridge University Press, 2009.

McKelway, Alexander J. *The Systematic Theology of Paul Tillich: A Review and Analysis*. Richmond, Va.: John Knox Press, 1964.

Musser, Donald W. "Theological Reasoning: A Tillichean Perspective." *The Whirlwind in Culture*. Edited by Donald W. Musser and Joseph L. Price. Bloomington, Ind.: Meyer-Stone Books, 1988.

———. "Tillich's Epistemology: An Assessment from a Post-Empiricist Standpoint." *Soundings* 69 (Winter 1986): 423–35.

Newport, John P. *Paul Tillich*. Makers of the Modern Theological Mind series. Edited by Bob E. Patterson. Waco: Word Books, 1984.

O'Meara, Thomas A., and C. D. Weisser, eds. *Paul Tillich in Catholic Thought*. Dubuque, Iowa: Priory Press, 1964.

Pauck, Wilhelm, and Marion Pauck. *Paul Tillich: His Life and Thought*. New York: Harper & Row, 1976.

Plaskow, Judith. *Sex, Sin and Grace: Women's Experience and the Theologies of Reinhold Niebuhr and Paul Tillich*. Lanham, Md.: University Press of America, 1980.

Price, Joseph L. "Expressionism and Ultimate Reality: Paul Tillich's Theology of Art." *Soundings* 69 (Winter 1986): 479–98.

———, with Truman Madsen. "A Dialogue on the Theology of Paul Tillich." *Mormonism in Dialogue with Contemporary Christian Theologies*. Edited by Donald W. Musser and David L. Paulsen. Macon, Ga.: Mercer University Press, 2007.

Romers, Joan Arnold. "The Protestant Principle: A Woman's Eye View of Barth and Tillich." Pages 319–40 in *Religion and Sexism: Images of Women in the Jewish and Christian Traditions*. Edited by Rosemary Radford Ruether. Eugene, Ore.: Wipf and Stock, 1998.

Rowe, W. *Religious Symbols and God: A Philosophical Study of Tillich's Theology*. Chicago: University of Chicago Press, 1968.

Scharlemann, Robert P. *Reflection and Doubt in the Thought of Paul Tillich*. New Haven: Yale University Press, 1969.

Stone, Ronald H. *Paul Tillich's Radical Social Thought*. Atlanta: John Knox Press, 1980.

IV. Bibliographic and Archival Resources

Tillich Archive. Andover-Harvard Theological Library, Harvard Divinity School, Cambridge, Mass. Online: http://oasis.harvard.edu/html/div00649.html.

Paul Tillich Audio Tape Collection. Union Theological Seminary, Richmond, Va. Online: http://learn.union-psce.edu/resources/Media%20Center/tapes.htm.

Extensive archival information is available in John J. Carey, *Paulus: Then and Now* (Macon, Ga.: Mercer University Press, 2002), 117–40.

NOTES

1. Life and Career

1. Of particular importance to Tillich's life and career is the volume by Wilhelm and Marion Pauck, *Paul Tillich: His Life and Thought* (New York: Harper & Row, 1976).

2. "To Be or Not to Be," *Time* (March 16, 1959): 46–52.

3. Jonathan Z. Smith, "Connections," *Journal of the American Academy of Religion* 58 (Winter 1990): 6.

4. "The Impact of Tillich's Interpretation of Religion," in *The Thought of Paul Tillich* (ed. James Luther Adams, Wilhelm Pauck, and Roger Shinn; San Francisco: Harper & Row, 1985), 258.

5. *FR*, 53.

2. Method and Symbols

1. *ST*, 1:46.

2. Paul Tillich, "Theology and Symbolism," in *Religious Symbolism* (edited by F. Ernest Johnson; New York: Harper and Brothers, 1955), 108.

3. *DF*, 45.

4. *TC*, 59.

5. *ST*, 1:28.

6. *ST*, 1:6.

7. *ST*, 1:21.

8. Ibid.

9. *ST*, 1:7.

10. *ST*, 1:8.

11. Mark Kline Taylor, *Paul Tillich: Theologian of the Boundaries* (London: Collins, 1987), 126–127; and *The Essential Tillich* (ed. F. Forrester Church; Chicago: University of Chicago Press, 1999).

12. *ST*, 1:61–62.

13. "Beyond Religious Socialism," *Christian Century* 66 (June 15, 1949): 733.

14. *ST*, 1:65.

15. *ST*, 1:12.

16. *ST*, 1:14.

17. *ST*, 1:21.

18. *ST*, 1:39.

19. *ST*, 1:46.

20. *ST*, 1:53.

21. Paul Tillich, "Religious Symbol," in *Myth and Symbol* (ed. F. W. Dillistone; London: SPCK, 1966), 15.

22. *DF*, 42.

23. "Theology and Symbolism," 109.

24. "Religious Symbol," 29.

25. "The Nature of Religious Language," 58–59.

26. Ibid., 59.

27. See *TPE*, 61.

28. "Theology and Symbolism," 110.
29. *DF*, 47.
30. *ST*, 1:240.
31. *DF*, 44–45.
32. "Theology and Symbolism," 108.
33. Ibid.
34. Ibid.
35. *DF*, 41.
36. "Theology and Symbolism," 111.
37. Ibid., 112.

3. Reason and the Quest for Revelation
1. *ST*, 1:118.
2. *ST*, 1:109.
3. *ST*, 1:73.
4. Ibid.
5. *ST*, 1:76.
6. *ST*, 1:77.
7. *ST*, 1:76.
8. *ST*, 1:77.
9. *ST*, 1:78.
10. *ST*, 1:79.
11. *ST*, 1:79–80.
12. *ST*, 1:80–83.
13. *ST*, 1:83.
14. *ST*, 1:84–85.
15. *ST*, 1:87–88.
16. *ST*, 1:89.
17. *ST*, 1:94.
18. MSFA, 67.
19. *ST*, 1:94.
20. *ST*, 1:95.
21. *ST*, 1:97.
22. *ST*, 1:98.
23. *ST*, 1:97. Tillich makes this point concisely in "Participation and Knowledge," in *Sociologica Frankfurter Beitrage zur Soziologie*, Band I (Hamburg: Europaische Verlagsanstalt, 1955), 201–209.
24. *ST*, 1:72–73.
25. *ST*, 1:73–74.
26. *ST*, 1:102.
27. Ibid.
28. *ST*, 1:105.
29. MSFA, 81.
30. MSFA, 80.
31. MSFA, 65–66.
32. Tillich, "Participation and Knowledge," 202.
33. Ibid., 206.
34. *ST*, 1:108.
35. *ST*, 1:110.
36. *ST*, 1:109.

37. *ST*, 1:111.
38. *ST*, 1:112.
39. *ST*, 1:112–113.
40. *ST*, 1:113.
41. Ibid.
42. *ST*, 1:116.
43. *ST*, 1:118.
44. *ST*, 1:122–126.
45. *ST*, 1:125.
46. *ST*, 1:128.
47. *ST*, 1:133.
48. Ibid.
49. *ST*, 1:134.
50. *ST*, 1:135.
51. *ST*, 1:135–136.
52. *ST*, 1:137–143.
53. The remainder of *ST* therefore expounds the meaning of Jesus as the Christ (part 3), life in the spiritual community (part 4), and actual living in the kingdom of God (part 5).
54. *ST*, 1:150–153.

4. Being and God

1. *SF*, 128.
2. *LPJ*, 108.
3. Paul Tillich, "Religious Symbol," in *Myth and Symbol* (ed. F. W. Dillistone; London: SPCK, 1966), 32–33.
4. *ST*, 1:206.
5. *ST*, 1:208.
6. *ST*, 1:211.
7. See *LPJ*, 25–34.
8. *ST*, 1:211.
9. *ST*, 1:214.
10. *TPE*, 63.
11. *SF*, 128.
12. Cf. John Dillenberger, "Tillich's Use of the Concept 'Being,'" *Christianity and Crisis* 13 (March 16, 1953): 30.
13. *ST*, 1:244.
14. *ST*, 1:243–244.
15. *BR*, 83.
16. *ST*, 1:245.
17. See lexicon entry, "God beyond God."
18. *ST*, 1:241–289.
19. *ST*, 1:241.
20. Hartshorne, "Tillich's Doctrine of God," in *The Theology of Paul Tillich* (ed. Charles Kegley and Robert Bretall; New York: Macmillan, 1952), 178.
21. *ST*, 1:245.
22. For examples, see Charles W. Kegley, *Politics, Religion, and Modern Man* (Quezon City, Philippines: University of Philippines Press, 1969), 81–82; and John F. Skinner, "A Critique of Tillich's Ontology," *Anglican Theological Review* 39 (1957): 57–58.

23. *SF*, 53.
24. *DF*, 45.
25. Cf. H. P. Owen, *Concepts of Deity* (New York: Herder and Herder, 1971), 129–132.
26. *ST*, 1:45–46.
27. *ST*, 1:215.
28. *ST*, 1:218.
29. *SF*, 42.
30. Tillich, "Religious Symbol," 32–33.
31. *SF*, 45.
32. *ST*, 1:237.
33. Cf. Christopher Kiesling, "A Translation of Tillich's Idea of God," *Journal of Ecumenical Studies* 4 (Fall 1967): 700–715.
34. *ST*, 1:238.
35. *ST*, 2:9.
36. *DF*, 45.
37. *ST*, 2:9.
38. *ST*, 2:10.
39. *DF*, 45.
40. *ST*, 1:244.
41. *ST*, 1:250.
42. Ibid.
43. *ST*, 1:250–251.
44. *ST*, 1:279.

5. Existence and New Being

1. *ST*, 1:67.
2. *ST*, 2:38.
3. *NB*, 15.
4. *ST*, 2:30.
5. *ST*, 2:56.
6. *ST*, 2:92.
7. *ST*, 2:123.
8. *ST*, 2:122.
9. *ST*, 2:158.
10. *ST*, 2:159–164.
11. *NB*, 20.
12. *NB*, 24.

6. Life, Its Ambiguities, and the Quest for Unambiguous Life

1. *DF*, 27.
2. *ST*, 3:3–110.
3. *ST*, 3:11–12.
4. *ST*, 3:12.
5. *ST*, 3:18–21.
6. *ST*, 3:20.
7. *ST*, 3:21.
8. *ST*, 3:22.
9. *ST*, 3:38.

10. *ST*, 3:51.
11. *ST*, 3:53.
12. *ST*, 3:66–67.
13. *ST*, 3:149–161.
14. Contemporary culture has seen a lively renewal of the appreciation of symbols as "pointers" to significant meanings in, for example, national flags, sacred places such as historic battlefields, and even the twin towers of September 11, 2001.
15. *DF*, 35–47.
16. *ST*, 2:137.
17. *CE*, 44–45. Tillich strongly agrees with Barth here, and he commends Barth's absolutist stand against the quasi-religious Nazi threats.
18. *CE*, 28–30.
19. *CE*, 33–34.
20. *CE*, 85–87.
21. *CE*, 89–92.
22. *CE*, 95.
23. *CE*, viii.
24. *CE*, 4.
25. Although the nationalism that evoked Tillich's interest was German Nazism and Soviet Communism, now long past, his thinking is important for theologians today who seek to understand fanatic commitments to national causes and attitudes of absolute obedience to national policies ("my country right or wrong"). One of the coauthors experienced a version of quasi-religious nationalism in what could be called military religion during his career in the United States Air Force. In military religion a person makes an absolute commitment to defend the national interest above all other commitments.

7. History and the Kingdom of God
1. *IH*, 264.
2. *ST*, 3:300.
3. *ST*, 3:302.
4. *ST*, 3:313.
5. *PE*, 152, emphasis added.
6. *IH*, 245.
7. *ST*, 3:327.
8. *ST*, 3:339.
9. *ST*, 3:348.
10. *ST*, 3:350.
11. *IH*, 243.
12. "Historical and Nonhistorical Interpretations of History: A Comparison," in *TPE*, 16–31.
13. *ST*, 3:359.
14. *ST*, 3:361.
15. *ST*, 3:363.
16. *IH*, 256–257.
17. *ST*, 3:364.
18. *ST*, 3:370.
19. *Ultimate Concern: Tillich in Dialogue* (ed. D. MacKenzie Brown; New York: Evanston, 1956), 126.
20. *ST*, 3:372.
21. *TPE*, 47.
22. Ibid.

23. See *PE*, 55.
24. *ST*, 1:267.
25. Ibid.
26. *SF*, 106.
27. *ST*, 3:378.
28. *ST*, 3:381.
29. *ST*, 3:383.
30. *ST*, 3:396.
31. *ST*, 3:397.
32. *ST*, 3:400.
33. Ibid.
34. *ST*, 3:400–401.
35. *ST*, 3:401.
36. See Tillich's essay "The Kingdom of God and History," in *The Kingdom of God and History*, The Official Oxford Conference Books (vol. 3, by H. G. Wood, C. H. Dodd, Edwyn Bevan, et al.; Chicago: Willett, Clark and Co., 1938), 115.

8. Faith and Truth
1. *DF*, 1.
2. *DF*, 18.
3. *SF*, 53.
4. *ST*, 1:211.
5. *DF*, 112.
6. *DF*, 81.
7. *DF*, 82.
8. *DF*, 86.
9. *DF*, 87.
10. *DF*, 88–89.
11. *DF*, 76–77.
12. *DF*, 77.
13. *DF*, 78–79.
14. *DF*, 79.
15. *DF*, 18.
16. *DF*, 16.
17. Cf. *CB*.
18. *SF*, 121.
19. *DF*, 20.
20. *NB*, 68.
21. *TPE*, 165–166.
22. *NB*, 69–70.
23. *NB*, 73.
24. *NB*, 72.
25. *NB*, 73–74.

9. Theology of Culture
1. *TC*, 42.
2. *DF*, 42.
3. *ST*, 3:5.
4. Ronald H. Stone, *Paul Tillich's Radical Social Thought* (Atlanta: John Knox Press, 1980), 134–135.

5. *WIR*, 160.

6. Ibid., 165.

7. John Dillenberger, "Paul Tillich: Theologian of Culture," in *Paul Tillich: Retrospect and Future* (Nels F. S. Ferré, Charles Hartshorne, John Dillinberger, et al.; Nashville: Abingdon Press, 1966), 32.

8. *TPE*, 63.

9. *PE*, 1.

10. Paul Tillich, "Church and Contemporary Culture," *World Christian Education* 9:2 (1956): 43.

11. *WIR*, 176–177.

12. Paul Tillich, "Theology, Architecture, and Art," *Church Management* 33 (October 1956): 7.

13. "Protestantism and the Contemporary Style in the Visual Arts," *The Christian Scholar* 40:4 (December 1957): 307.

14. "The World Situation," in *The Christian Answer* (ed. Henry P. Van Dusen; New York: Charles Scribner's Sons, 1945), 11.

15. "Religiöser Stil und religiöser Stoff in der bildenden Kunst," quoted in *Paul Tillich's Philosophy of Culture, Science, and Religion* by James Luther Adams (New York: Harper and Row, Publishers, 1965), 81.

16. "Theology and Symbolism," in *Religious Symbolism* (ed. F. Ernest Johnson; New York: Harper and Brothers, 1955), 109.

17. Paul Tillich, "Art and Ultimate Reality," *Cross Currents* 10 (Winter 1960): 2.

18. Paul Tillich, "Existentialist Aspects of Modern Art," in *Christianity and the Existentialists* (ed. Carl Michalson; New York: Charles Scribner's Sons, 1956), 145.

19. *RS*, 85.

20. Paul Tillich, *The Spiritual Situation in Our Technical Society* (ed. J. Mark Thomas; Macon, Ga.: Mercer University Press, 1988), 151–152.

21. Ibid., 162.

22. Ibid., 163.

23. "Science and Theology: A Discussion with Einstein," in *TC*, 129.

24. "Reformations" in science were possible because science has its own version of the Protestant principle.

25. Paul Tillich, "Moralisms and Morality: Theonomous Ethics," in *Ministry and Medicine in Human Relations* (ed. Iago Galdston; New York: International Universities Press, Inc., 1955).

26. Ibid., 396.

27. Ibid.

28. *MB*, 14.

29. Tillich expounds on morality in *MB* and *LPJ*.

30. See Schweiker's foreword to *MB*, 1–10.

31. See John J. Carey, *Paulus: Then and Now* (Macon, Ga.: Mercer University Press, 2002), 103–16, for an assessment of Tillich's ethics. Carey describes Tillich's views as an ethics of "self-realization." His treatment also addresses the disjunctures of Tillich's personal life and provides substantive bibliographic prompts.

32. Stone points out that Tillich's critique of capitalism was subdued in the United States, where social conditions were different (*Tillich's Radical Social Thought*, 71).

33. Ibid., 54–62.

10. Abiding Contributions

1. Michael Gazzaniga, in dialogue with Tom Wolfe, in "The Seed Salon," *Seed: Science Is Culture* 17 (July/August 2008): 42.

2. John J. Carey, *Paulus: Then and Now* (Macon, Ga.: Mercer University Press, 2002), 108.

INDEX